SIMPLE SONGS

The Easiest Easy Drum Songbook Ever

ISBN 978-1-4950-9977-9

HAL•LEONARD®

7777 W. BLUEMOUND RD. P.O. BOX 13819 MILWAUKEE, WI 53213

Visit Hal Leonard Online at
www.halleonard.com

Another Brick in the Wall, Part 2

Words and Music by Roger Waters

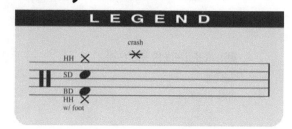

Verse
Moderately ♩ = 104

We don't need no ed - u - ca - tion...

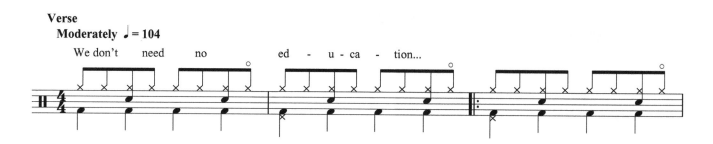

Play 5 times

To Coda $\oplus$

D.C. al Coda
(take repeats)

$\oplus$ **Coda**

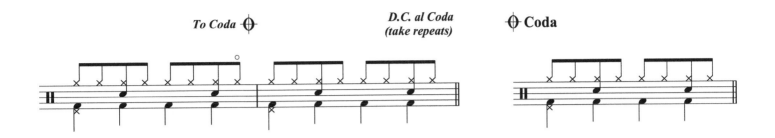

Guitar Solo

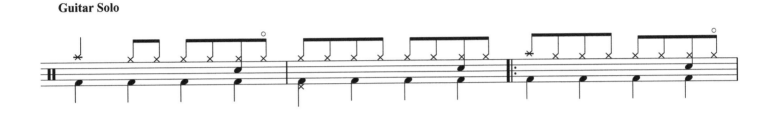

Play 10 times

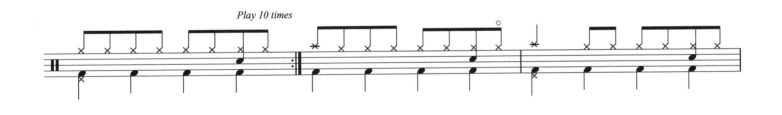

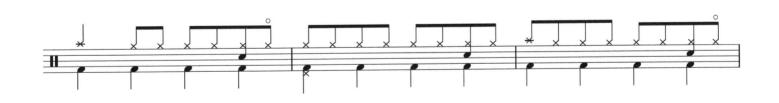

Repeat and fade

Outro

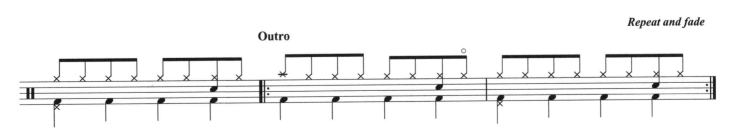

Another One Bites the Dust

Words and Music by John Deacon

Intro
Moderate Rock ♩ = 110

Play 5 times

Verse

Steve walks war - i - ly down   the   street...

Play 7 times

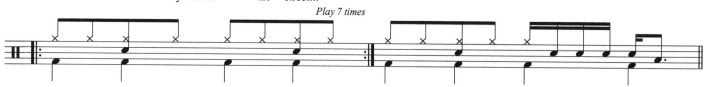

Chorus

An - oth - er   one   bites   the   dust...

Play 6 times

Verse

How do you think   I'm gon - na get a - long...

Play 7 times

Chorus

An - oth - er one bites the dust...

Interlude

Bridge

Verse

There are plen - ty of ways that you can hurt a man...

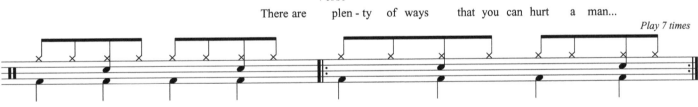

Chorus

An - oth-er one bites the dust...

Outro

Shoot - out!...

Back in Black

Words and Music by Angus Young,
Malcolm Young and Brian Johnson

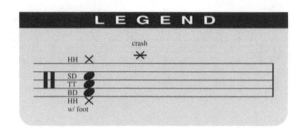

2nd time, substitute Fill 2

3rd time, substitute Fill 4

'Cause I'm   back.   Yes, I'm

back...

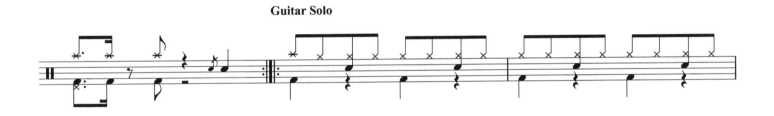

To Coda ⊕

2nd time, substitute Fill 3

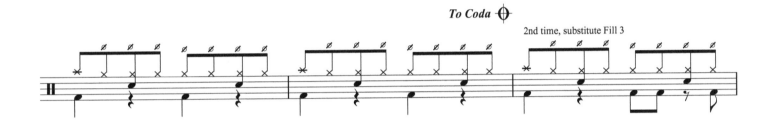

Guitar Solo

Play 3 times

Fill 2

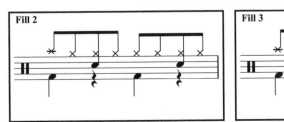

Fill 3

Fill 4

Well, I'm

⊕ Coda

Interlude

Chorus

Well, I'm   back...

back   in   black.

Play 3 times

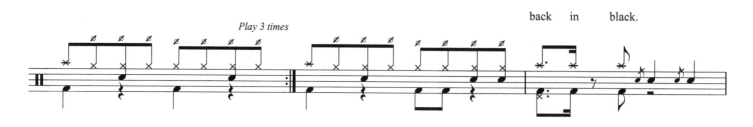

Outro

I wan-na say it.

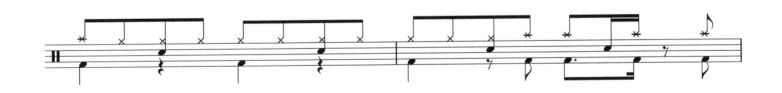

Fade out

Billie Jean

Words and Music by Michael Jackson

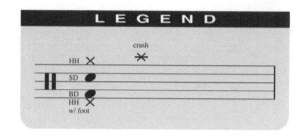

Intro
Moderate Pop ♩ = 117

Verse

She was more like a beau-

ty queen...

Pre-Chorus

Peo-ple al - ways told me, be care-ful of what you do...

Chorus

Bil - lie Jean is not my lov - er...

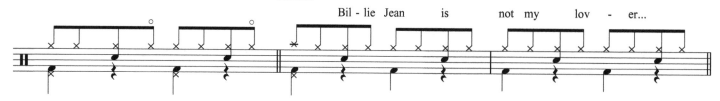

For for - ty days and for for - ty nights...

Play 4 times

She told my ba - by we danced till three...

Pre-Chorus

Peo-ple al - ways told me, be care-ful of what you do...

Play 3 times

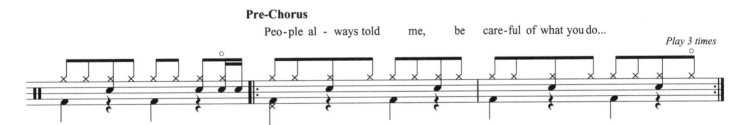

Chorus

Bil - lie Jean is

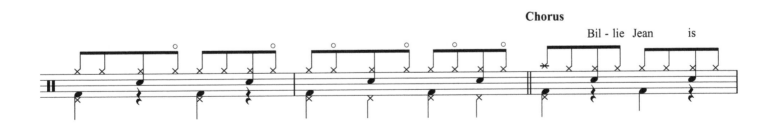

not my lov - er...

Play 4 times

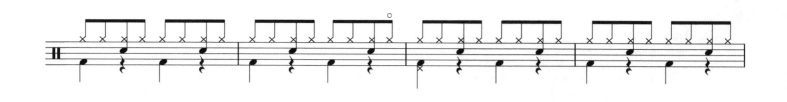

Interlude

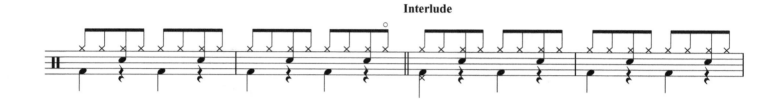

She says I   am the one...

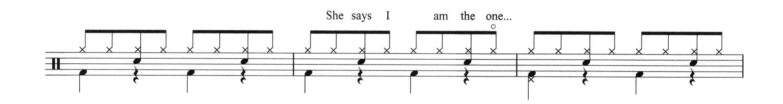

Chorus

Bil-lie Jean   is

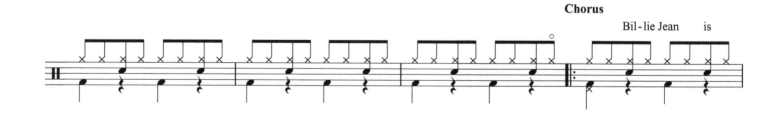

Repeat and fade

not my lov - er...

Black

Words by Eddie Vedder
Music by Stone Gossard

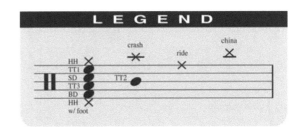

Pre-Chorus

Oh, and all I taught her was ev-'ry-thing...

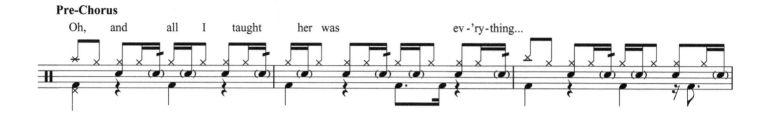

Chorus

And now my bit-ter hands...

D.S. al Coda

Play 3 times

○ **Coda**

Pre-Chorus

Ho, and twist-ed thoughts that spin 'round my head...

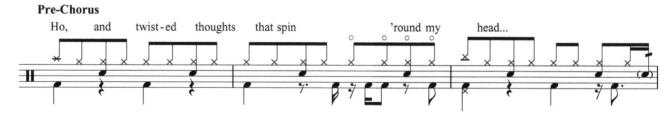

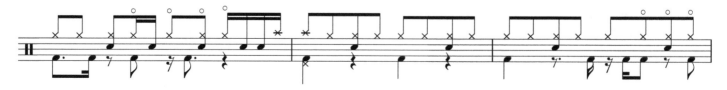

Chorus

And now   my bit-ter   hands...

Play 5 times

Interlude

know some - day you'll have   a   beau - ti - ful   life...

Outro

Do, do, do, do,   do, do, do...

Begin fade

Fade out

Brass in Pocket

Words and Music by Chrissie Hynde and James Honeyman-Scott

Intro
Moderate Rock ♩ = 98

Verse

I got brass — in pock - et...

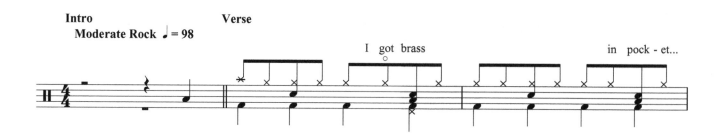

Verse

Got mo - tion, — re - strained e - mo - tion...

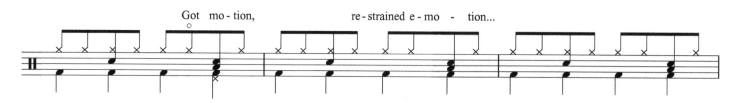

Gon - na use my

arms,   gon - na use my   legs...

Chorus

'Cause   I'm   gon - na make you   see...

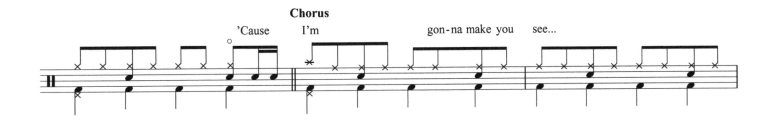

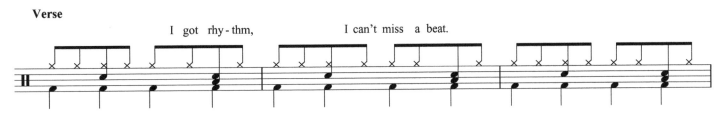

Verse

I got rhy - thm,   I can't miss a beat.

Pre-Chorus

Gon-na use my

arms, gon-na use my legs...

Chorus

I'm gon-na make you see...

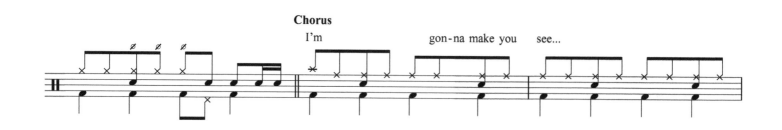

Outro

Centuries

Words and Music by Peter Wentz, Patrick Stump,
Joseph Trohman, Andrew Hurley, Jonathan Rotem,
Suzanne Vega, Justin Tranter, Michael Fonseca and Raja Kumari

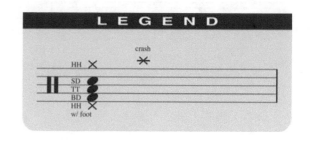

Chorus

Play 3 times

To Coda ⊕

Verse

I   can't   stop till the whole world...

D.S. al Coda
(take repeat)

Coda

Bridge

Chorus

1. | 2.

Outro

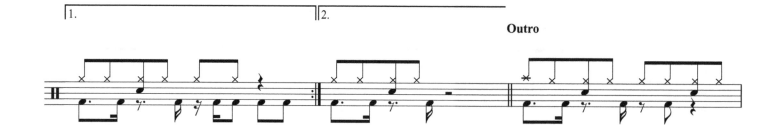

Come As You Are

Words and Music by Kurt Cobain

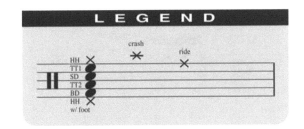

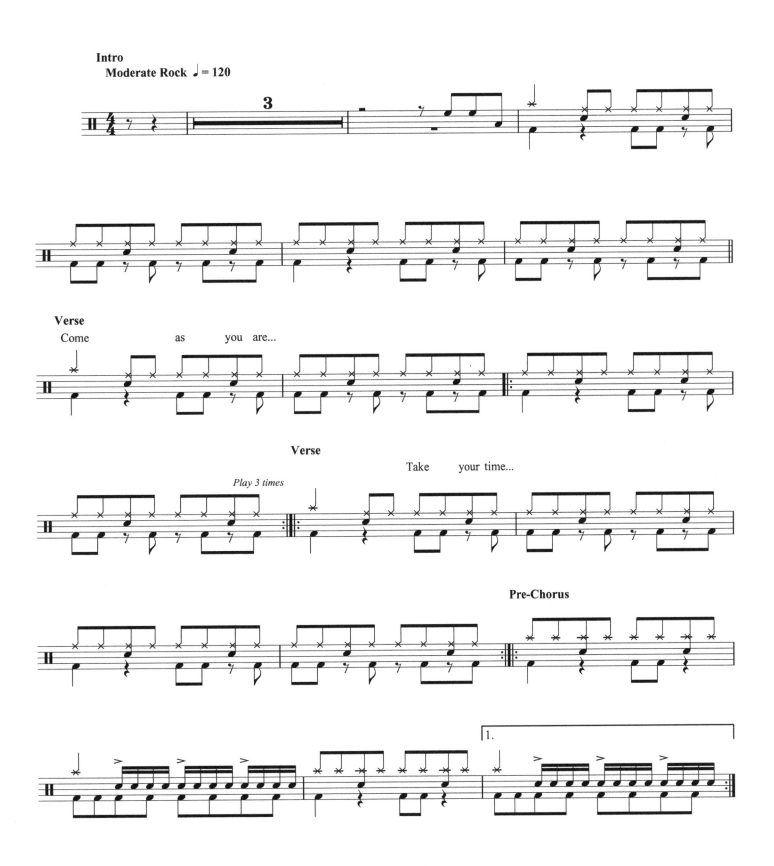

Verse

Come   doused   in mud...

Pre-Chorus

Play 3 times

Play 3 times

Chorus

And   I   swear   that   I...

Guitar Solo

Play 8 times

Pre-Chorus

Counting Stars

Words and Music by Ryan Tedder

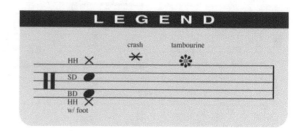

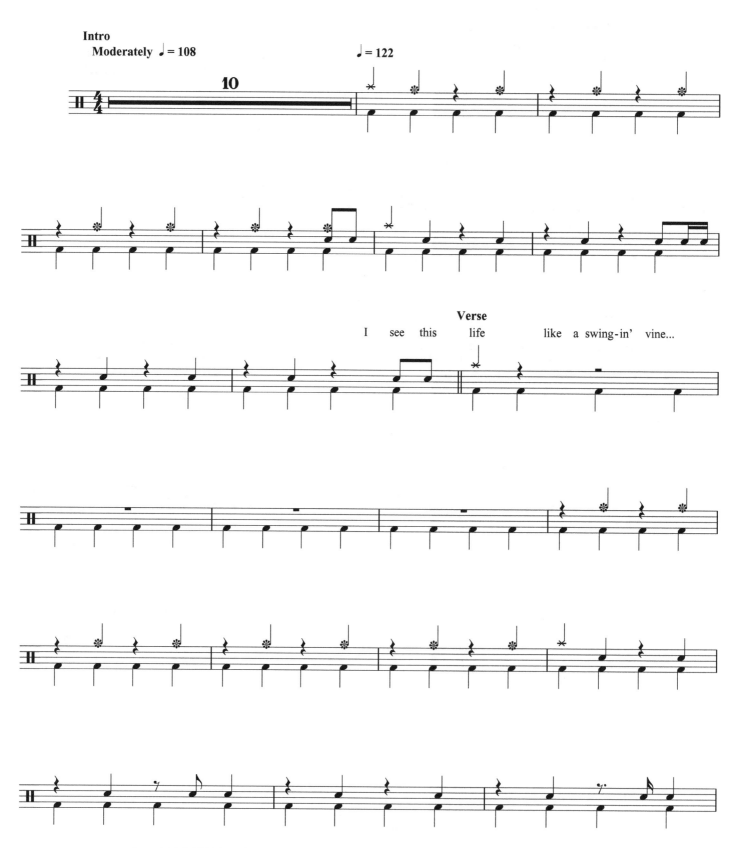

Chorus

Late - ly   I   been,

I   been los-in' sleep...

Verse

I feel your   love,   and I feel it burn...

%Chorus

Late - ly   I   been,   I been los - in' sleep...

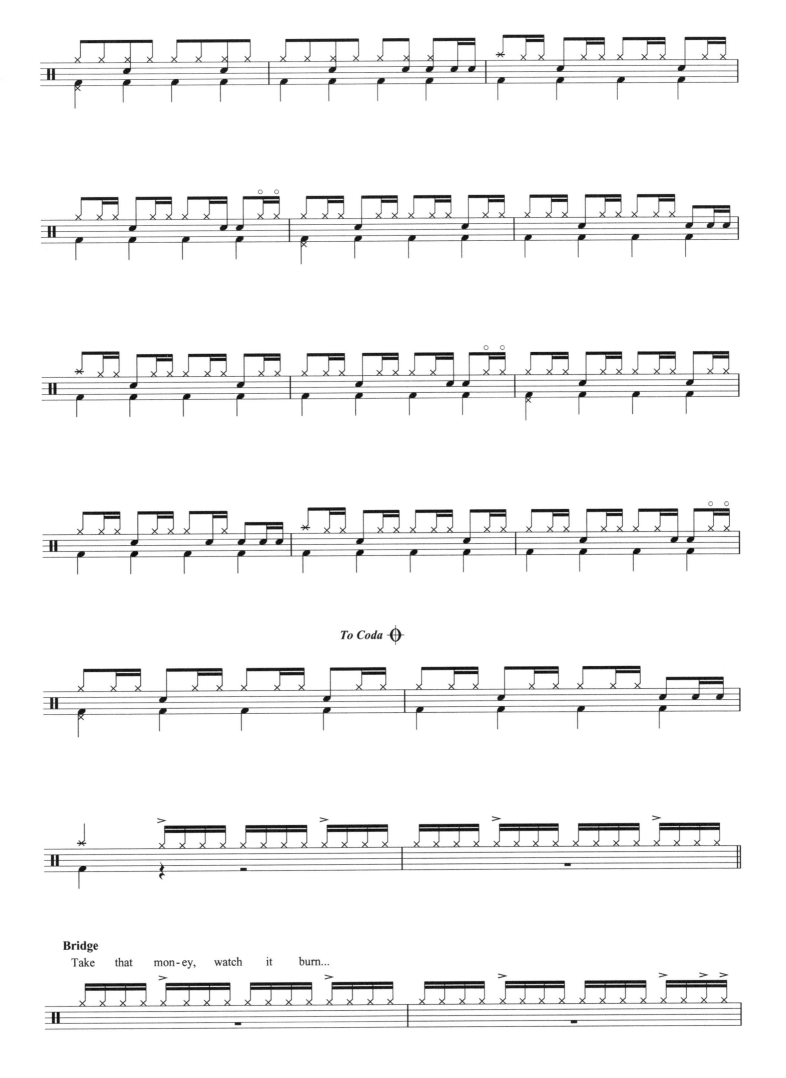

To Coda ⊕

Bridge

Take that mon-ey, watch it burn...

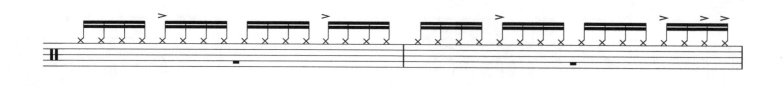

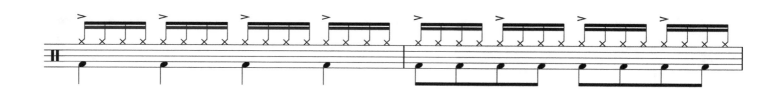

Ev - 'ry - thing that kills me   makes me feel a - live.

D.S. al Coda

Coda

Outro
Take that mon- ey, watch it burn.   Sink

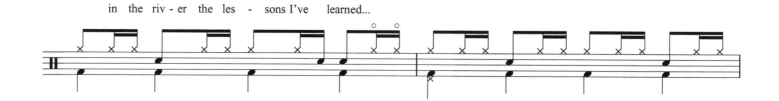

in the riv - er the les - sons I've learned...

1.   2.

Creep

Words and Music by Albert Hammond, Mike Hazlewood,
Thomas Yorke, Jonathan Greenwood, Colin Greenwood,
Edward O'Brien and Philip Selway

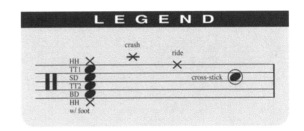

Verse

I don't care if it hurts...

Chorus

...but I'm a creep...

Bridge

She's   run - ning out   a - gain...

Verse

What - ev - er makes you hap - py...

Outro

Play 3 times

Play 5 times

rit.

37

Eye of the Tiger

Theme from ROCKY III

Words and Music by Frank Sullivan and Jim Peterik

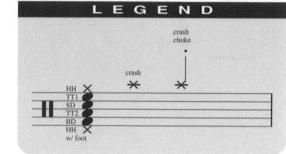

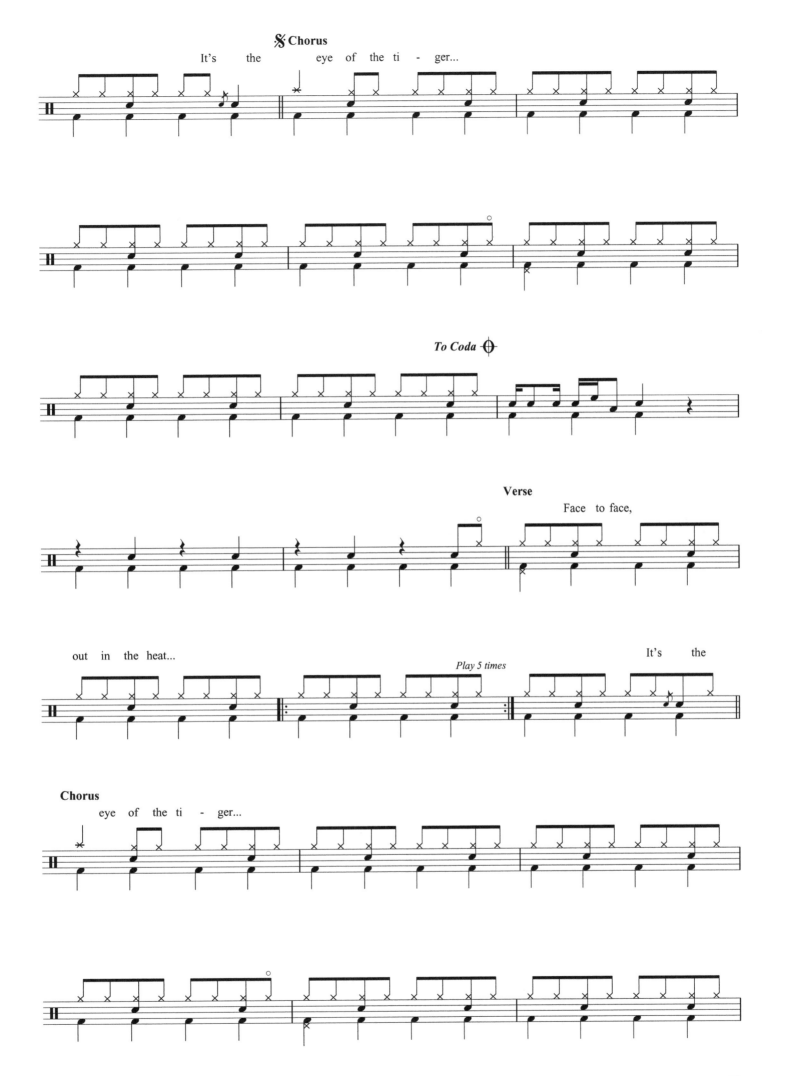

Verse

Ris - in' up,   straight to the top...

Play 5 times

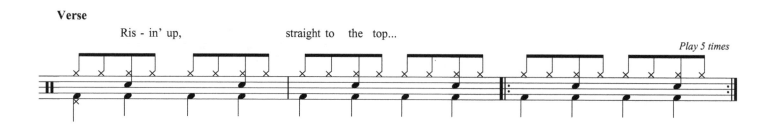

D.S. al Coda   **Coda**

It's   the

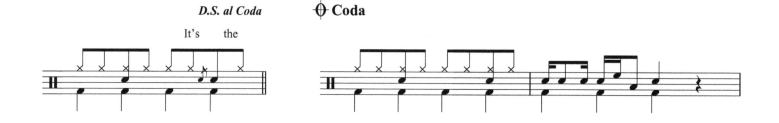

Outro

Begin fade

The eye of the ti -

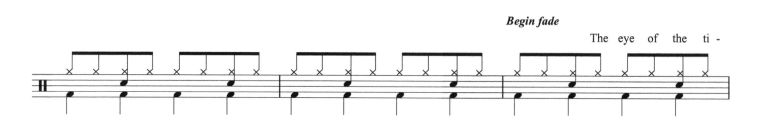

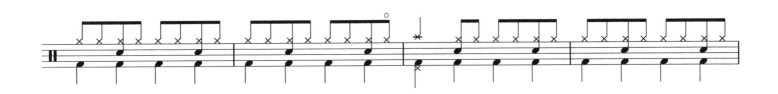

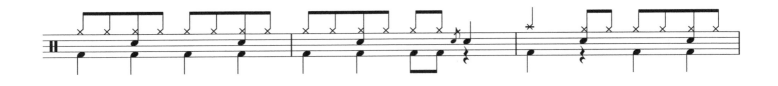

Fade out

Crossfire

Words and Music by Bill Carter, Ruth Ellsworth,
Reese Wynans, Tommy Shannon and Chris Layton

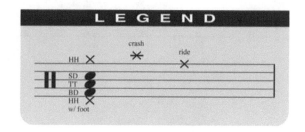

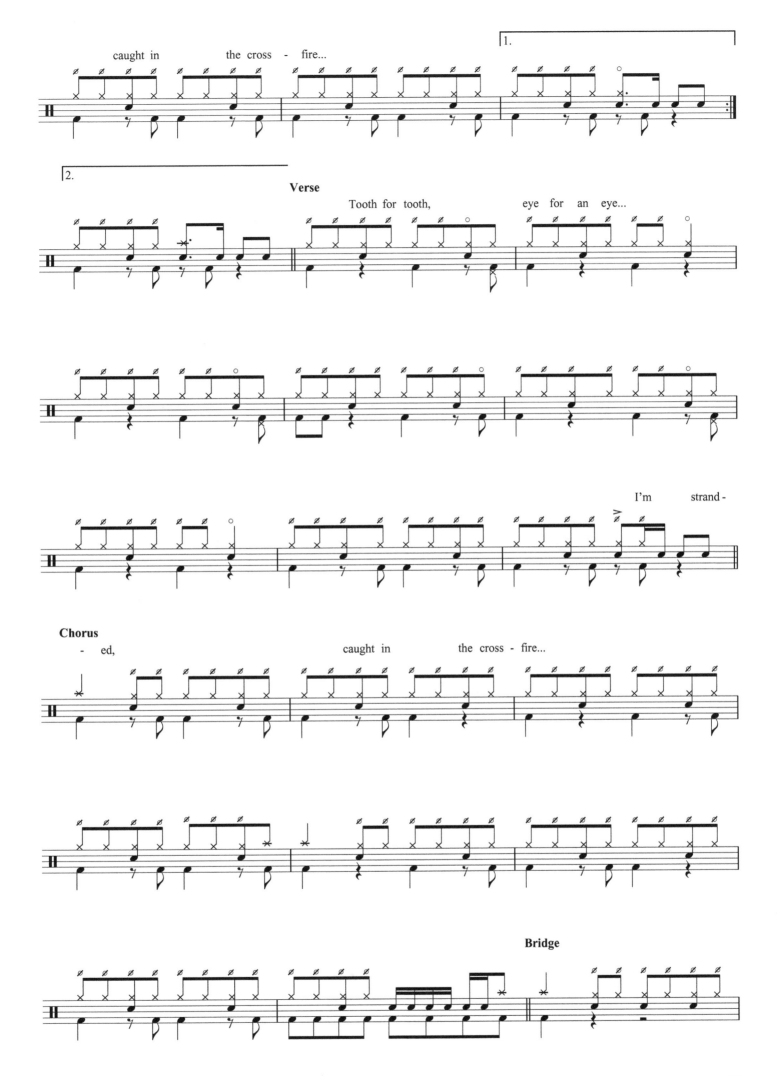

...we're

Chorus
strand - ed,   caught   in   the   cross - fire...

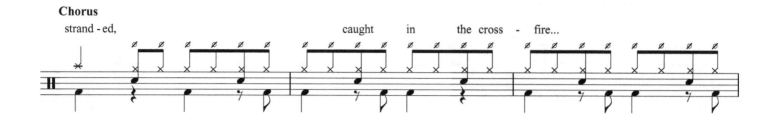

Guitar Solo
Play 6 times

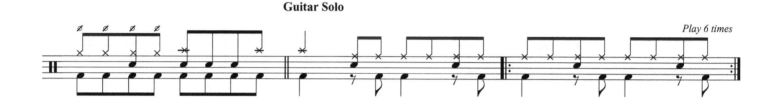

Verse

Save the strong,

lose the weak...

Chorus

We got strand - ed,   caught in   the cross -

- fire...

Outro-Guitar Solo

Day Tripper

Words and Music by John Lennon and Paul McCartney

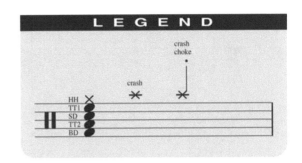

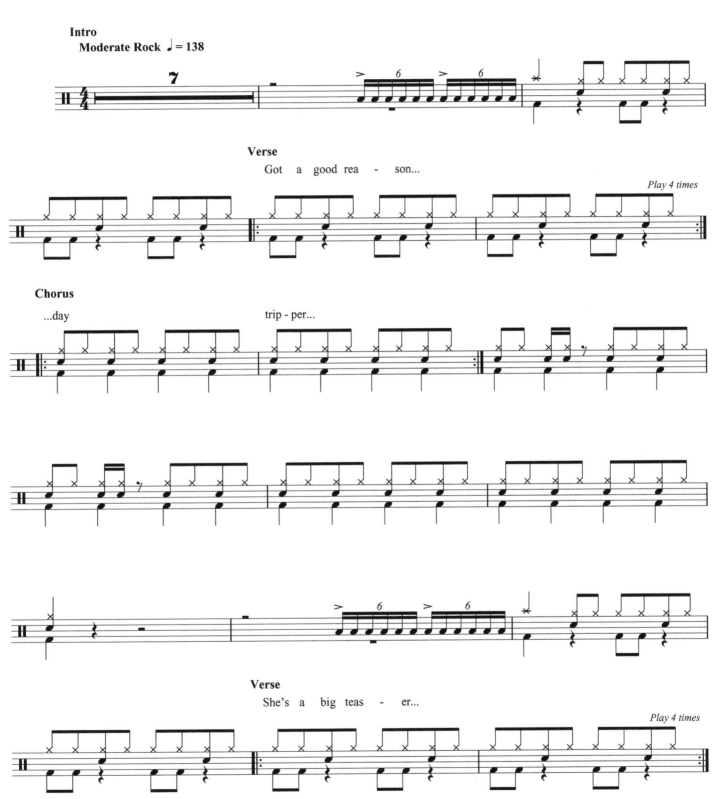

Chorus

...day   trip - per...

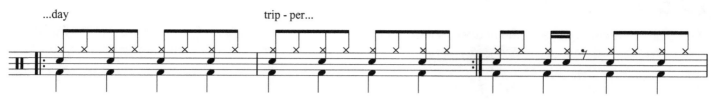

Interlude

Guitar Solo

Breakdown

Play 3 times

Verse

Tried   to please   her...

Play 3 times

Chorus

...day   trip - per...

Breakdown

Outro-Chorus

Day   trip - per...

Begin fade

Fade out

867-5309/Jenny

Words and Music by Alex Call and James Keller

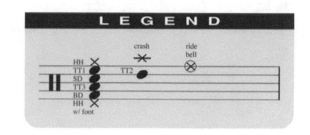

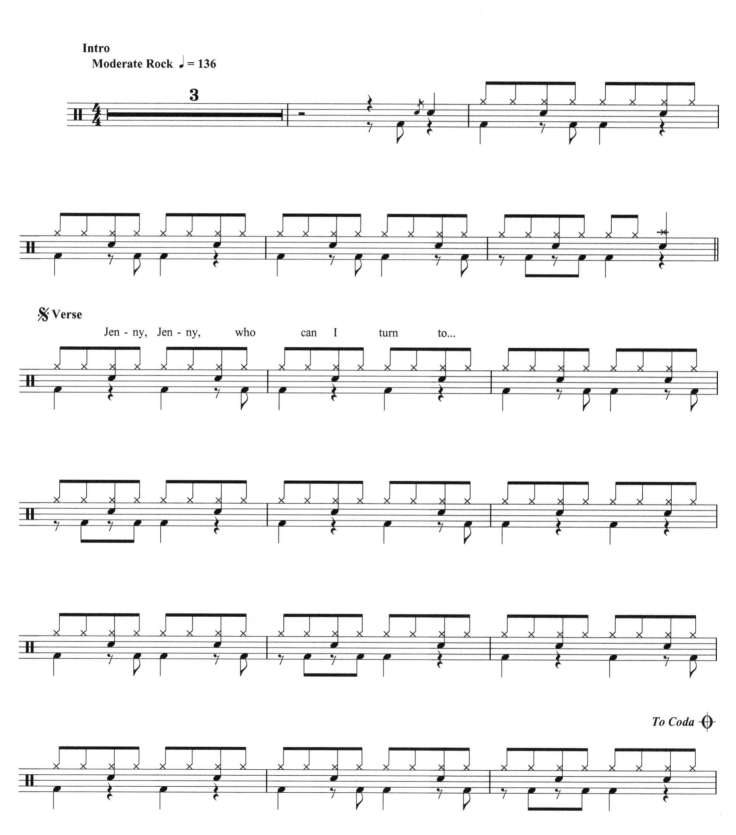

Pre-Chorus

Jen - ny, I've got your num - ber...

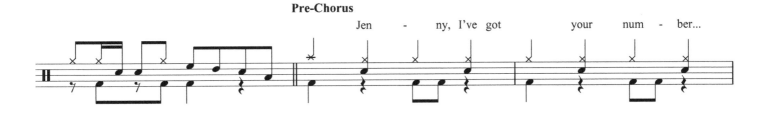

Chorus

Eight   Six   Sev - en Five   Three "O"   Nine...

D.S. al Coda   ⊕ **Coda**

Guitar Solo

Pre-Chorus

Jen - ny, don't change your num - ber...

Chorus

Eight Six Sev - en Five Three "O" Nine...

Outro-Chorus

Jen-ny, Jen-ny, who can I turn to...

Begin fade

Fade out

Fight for Your Right
(To Party)

Words and Music by Rick Rubin, Adam Horovitz and Adam Yauch

LEGEND

Intro
Moderately fast ♩ = 134

Kick it!

1. 2. You

Verse
wake up late for school, man, you don't...

1., 2., 3. 4.

Chorus
You got - ta fight...

Verse
Your pops caught you smok - ing, man, he...

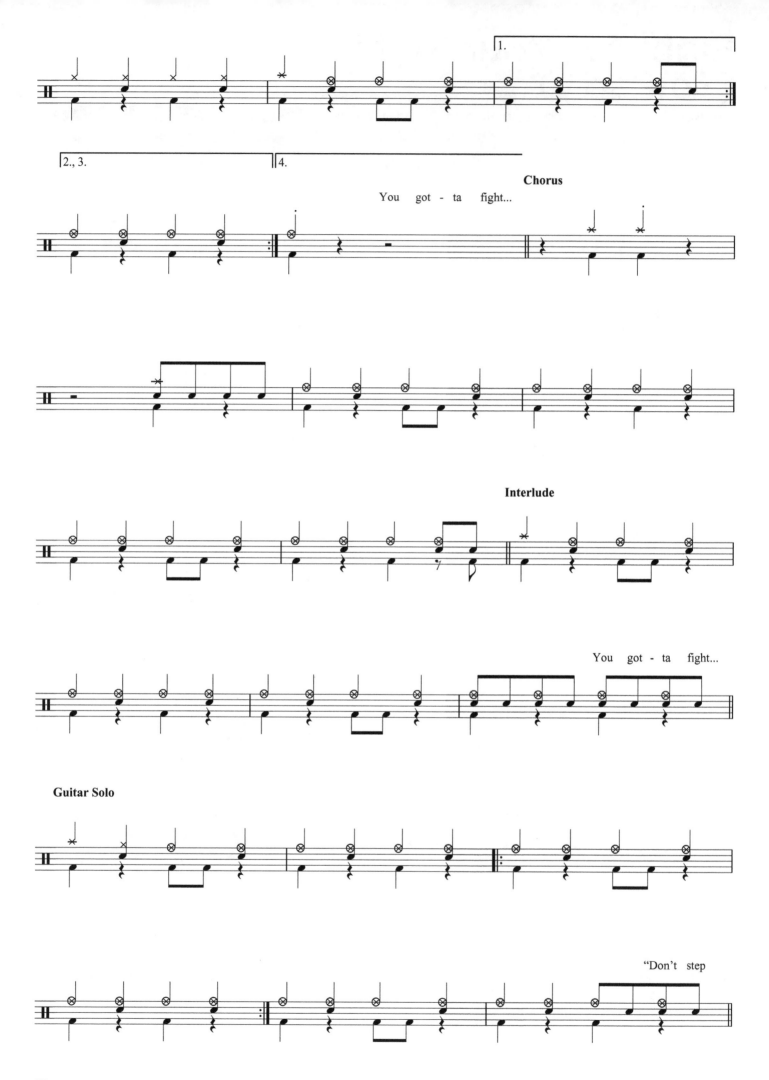

Chorus

You got - ta fight...

Interlude

You got - ta fight...

Guitar Solo

"Don't step

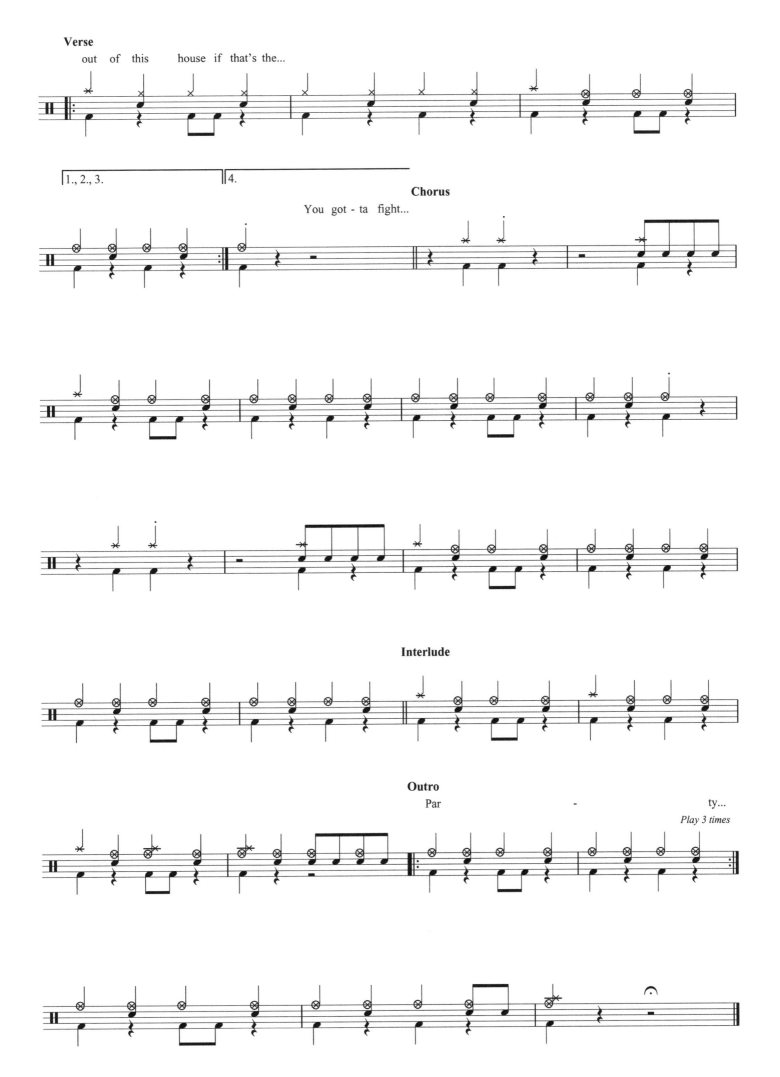

Verse

out of this house if that's the...

Chorus

You got - ta fight...

Interlude

Outro

Par - ty...

Play 3 times

Gimme Some Lovin'

Words and Music by Steve Winwood,
Muff Winwood and Spencer Davis

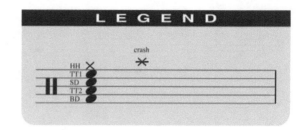

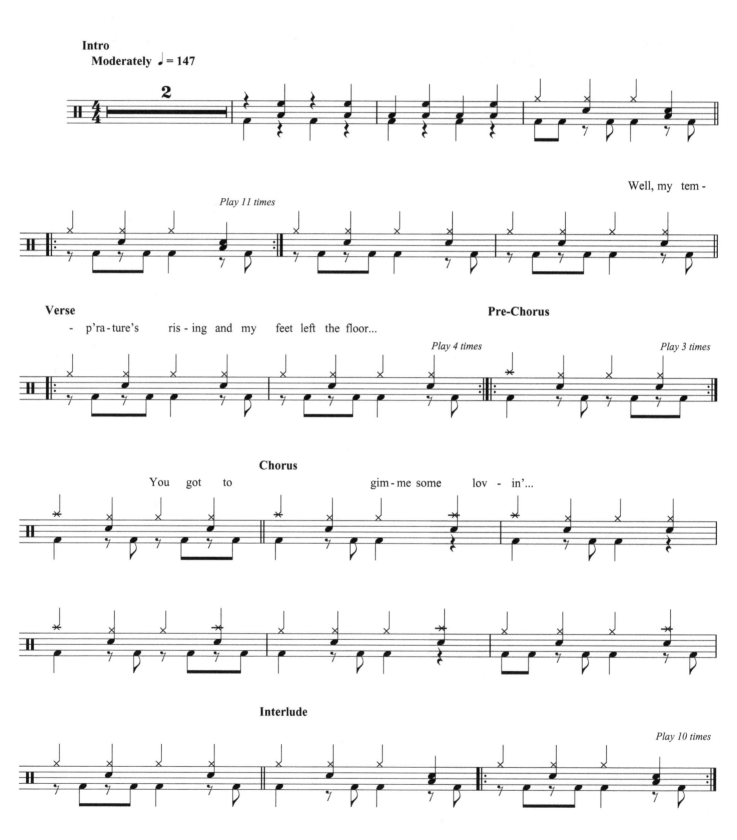

Verse

Well, I feel so good, ev - 'ry -

Pre-Chorus

thing is get - ting hot...

Play 4 times   *Play 3 times*

You got to

Chorus

gim - me some lov - in'...

Play 4 times

Interlude

Play 8 times

Verse

Well, I feel so good, ev - 'ry -

Pre-Chorus

thing is get - ting hot...

Play 4 times   *Play 3 times*

You got to

Chorus

gim - me some lov - in'...

Repeat and fade

Highway to Hell

Words and Music by Angus Young, Malcolm Young and Bon Scott

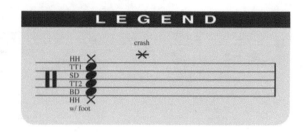

61

I'm on the

Play 3 times

Outro-Chorus

high - way to hell...

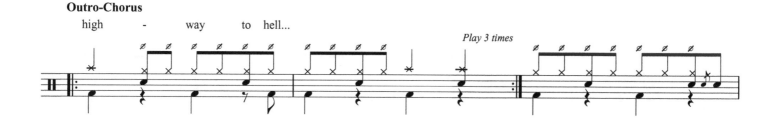

Play 3 times

Free time

mp ———————— *f*

How You Remind Me

Words by Chad Kroeger
Music by Nickelback

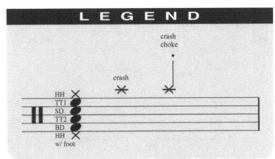

Verse

It's not like   you did-n't know that...

Chorus

It's not like you   to say sor - ry...

Play 3 times

Interlude   **Verse**

This is how   you re-mind

3   **4**

me...

Chorus

It's not like you   to say sor - ry...

Repeat and fade

I Love Rock 'N Roll

Words and Music by Alan Merrill and Jake Hooker

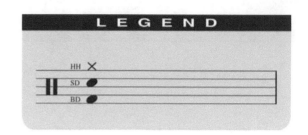

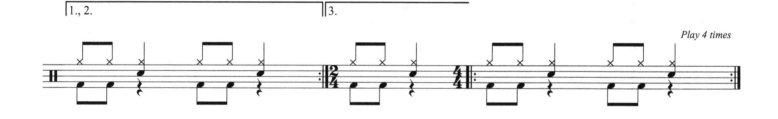

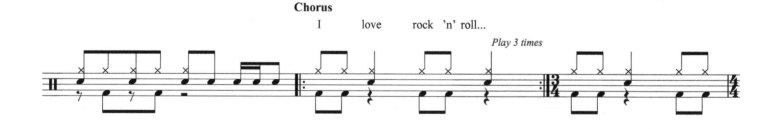

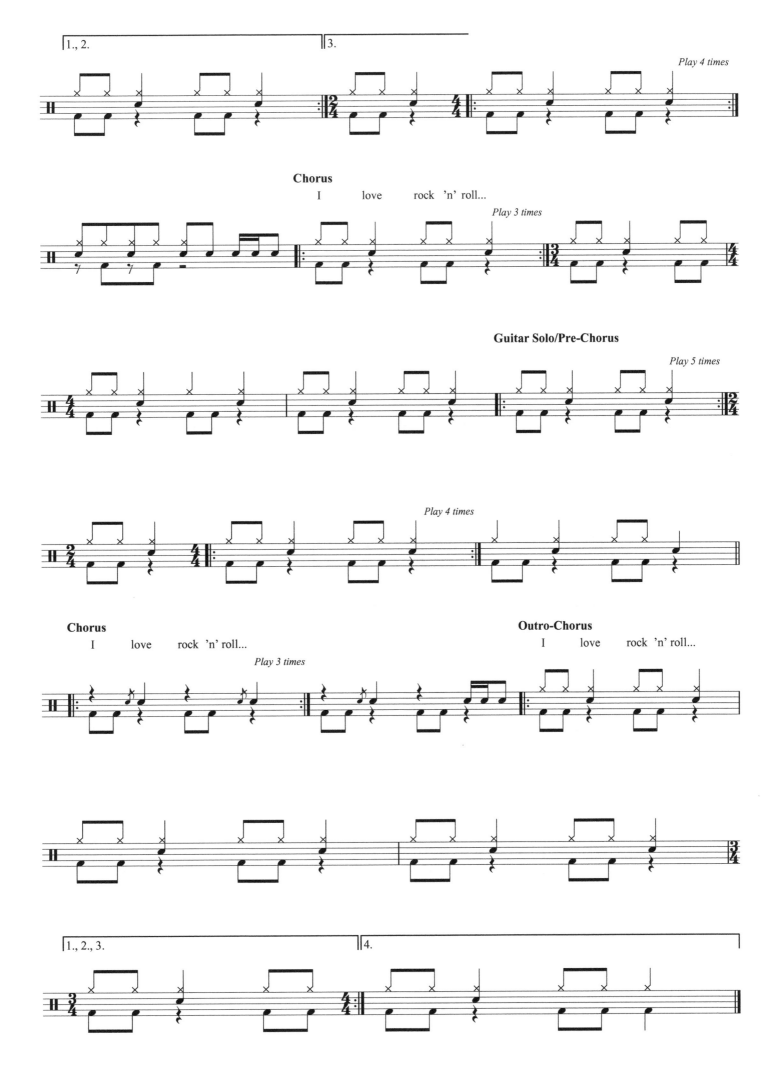

Chorus

I love rock 'n' roll...

Guitar Solo/Pre-Chorus

Chorus

I love rock 'n' roll...

Outro-Chorus

I love rock 'n' roll...

I Wanna Be Sedated

Words and Music by Jeffrey Hyman,
John Cummings and Douglas Colvin

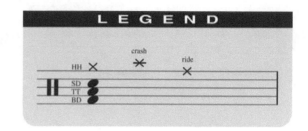

2nd time, substitute Fill 2

2nd time, substitute Fill 2

1.

2.

Interlude

Play 7 times

Verse

Twen - ty, twen - ty, twen - ty - four

2nd time, substitute Fill 3

hours   to   go...

Chorus

Just   put me in a wheel - chair...

Fill 2

Fill 3

2nd time, substitute Fill 4

1.

2.

Outro

Ba,   ba,   ba, ba,   ba,   ba,   ba, ba...

Fill 4

Jessie's Girl

Words and Music by Rick Springfield

Chorus

You know, I wish that I had Jes-sie's girl...

Interlude

Bridge

And I'm look-in' in the mir -

- ror all the time...

Interlude

Play 3 times

Guitar Solo

Chorus

You know, I wish that I had Jes - sie's girl...

Island in the Sun

Words and Music by Rivers Cuomo

Knock on Wood

Words and Music by Eddie Floyd and Steve Cropper

Intro
Moderately ♩ = 105

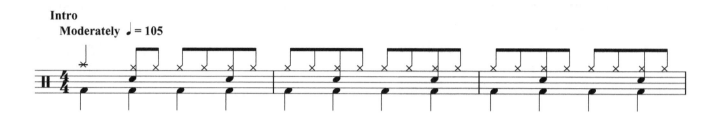

Verse

I don't wan - na lose this good thing...

Play 5 times

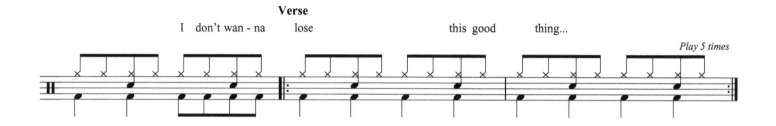

Chorus

It's like thun - der, light -

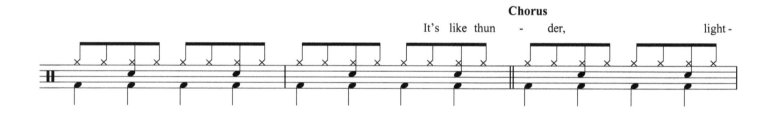

- nin'...

I'm not su - per - sti - tious   a - bout

you...   It's like thun -

Play 5 times

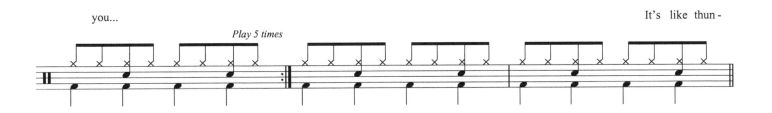

Chorus

- der,   light - nin'...

Interlude

Verse

It's no   se - cret,   that wom - an,

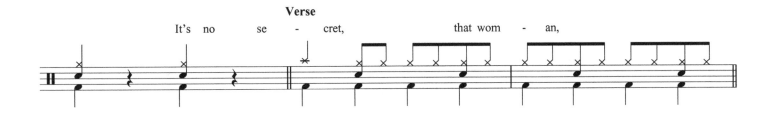

Play 4 times

Chorus

It's like thun - der, light - nin'...

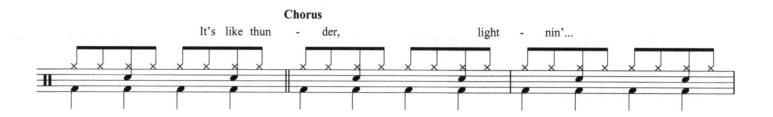

Outro

Repeat and fade

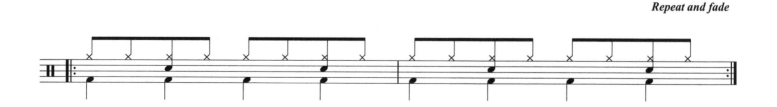

80

Learning to Fly

Words and Music by Tom Petty and Jeff Lynne

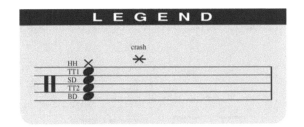

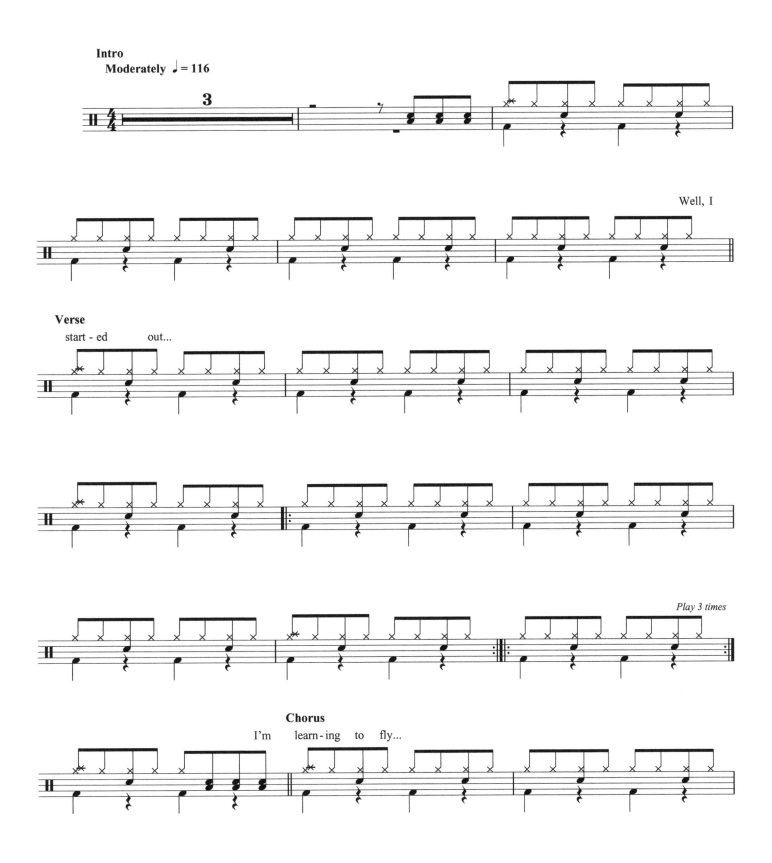

Verse
Well, the good old days...

Chorus
I'm learn-ing to fly...

To Coda

Guitar Solo

1.

2.
Well,

Kryptonite

Words and Music by Matt Roberts,
Brad Arnold and Todd Harrell

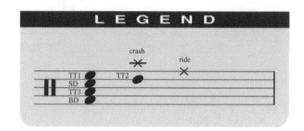

Intro
Fast Rock ♩ = 198

(Guitar)

Play 7 times

Verse

Well, I took a walk a - round the world...

Play 6 times

Interlude

Play 6 times

Verse

I watched the world float to the dark...

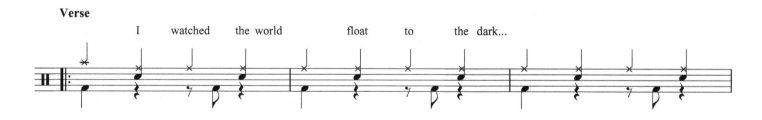

Chorus

If   I   go   cra - zy,   then   will...

Fill 1

Interlude

Chorus

If I go cra - zy, then will...

If   I   go   cra - zy,   then   will...

Interlude

Play 3 times

Let's Get It On

Words and Music by Marvin Gaye and Ed Townsend

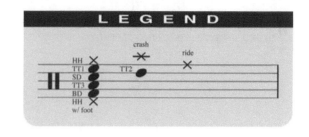

peo - ple...

Verse
There's   noth - in' wrong   with me...

Bridge
Don't you   know   how sweet and...

Chorus

Bridge

Come on,   come on,   come on,   come on,   come on   dar - lin'...

Chorus

Fade out

91

Like a Stone

Lyrics by Chris Cornell
Music written and arranged by Audioslave

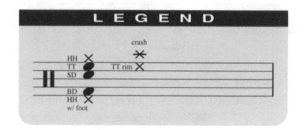

Intro
Moderately ♩ = 108

On a

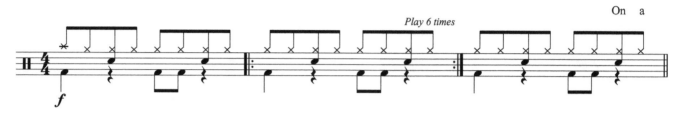

Verse
cob - web...

Chorus
In   your   house   I

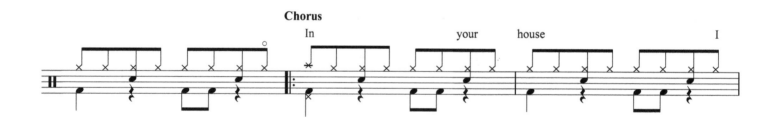

long   to   be...

Verse

And on my death - bed...

Play 6 times

Chorus

In your house I

long to be...

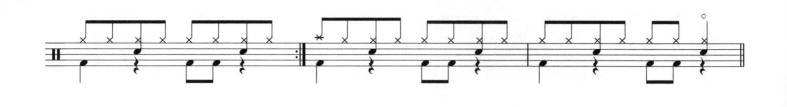

Guitar Solo

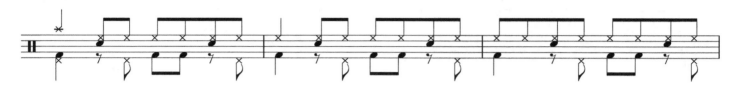

Bridge

And   on   I read   un -

til   the day   was   gone...

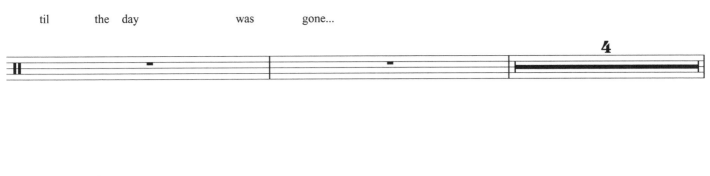

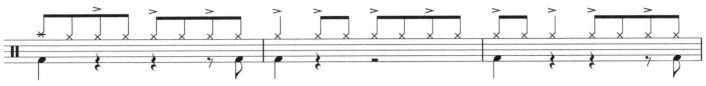

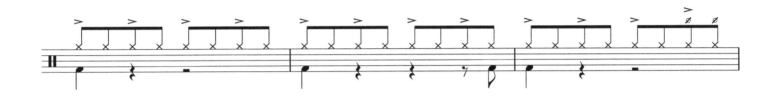

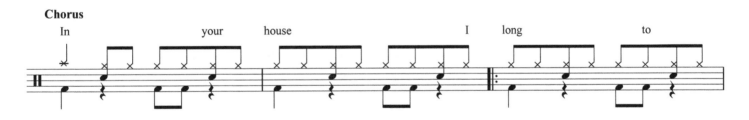

Chorus

In   your house   I long   to

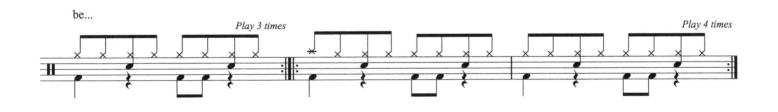

be...

Play 3 times   *Play 4 times*

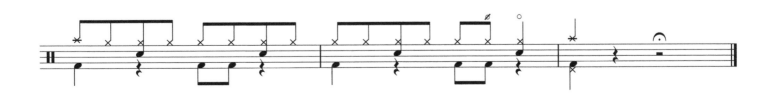

Living After Midnight

Words and Music by Glenn Raymond Tipton,
Robert Halford and Kenneth Downing

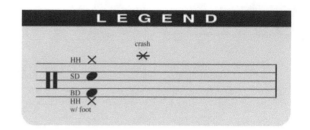

Intro
Moderate Rock ♩ = 134

Chorus

Liv - in'   af - ter   mid - night...

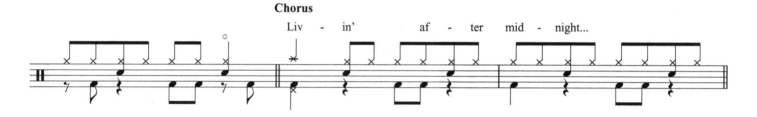

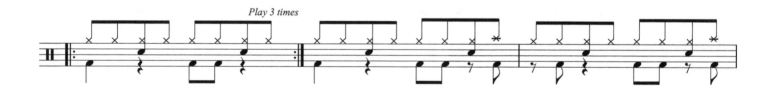

𝄋 **Verse**

I took the cit - y 'bout a   one A.   M....

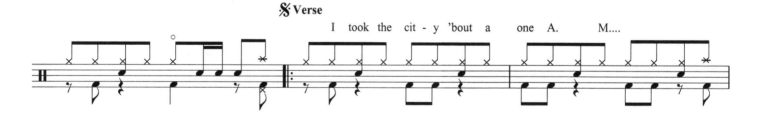

Pre-Chorus

I come a - live   in the   ne - on   lights...

Chorus

2nd time, substitute Fill 1

Liv - in'   af - ter   mid - night...

1.

2.

Bridge

Fill 1

Guitar Solo

D.S. al Coda   ⊕ **Coda**

𝄋𝄋 **Outro-Chorus**

Liv - in'   af - ter   mid - night...

D.S.S. and fade

Livin' on a Prayer

Words and Music by Jon Bon Jovi,
Desmond Child and Richie Sambora

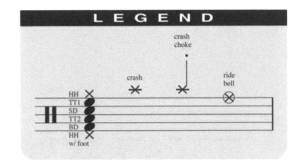

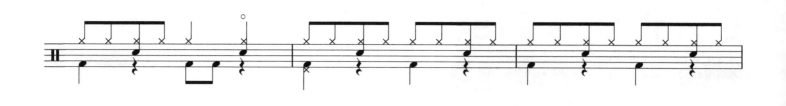

She says we've got to

Gradually open

Pre-Chorus

hold   on   to what we've got...

Chorus

Whoa,   we're half - way   there...

Whoa,   we're   half - way   there...

Guitar Solo

Whoa,   we're half - way   there...

Begin fade

Fade out

Man in the Box

Written by Jerry Cantrell and Layne Staley

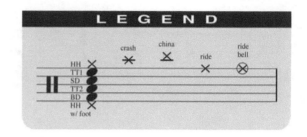

To Coda ⊕

1.

2.

Guitar Solo

D.S. al Coda   ⊕ **Coda**

Interlude

Ah,   ah,   ah...

My Friends

Words and Music by Anthony Kiedis, Flea,
Chad Smith and David Navarro

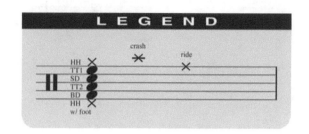

Coda

Chorus

I love all of you...

Outro

Play 3 times

rit.

Old Time Rock & Roll

Words and Music by George Jackson and Thomas E. Jones III

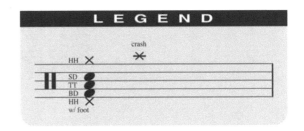

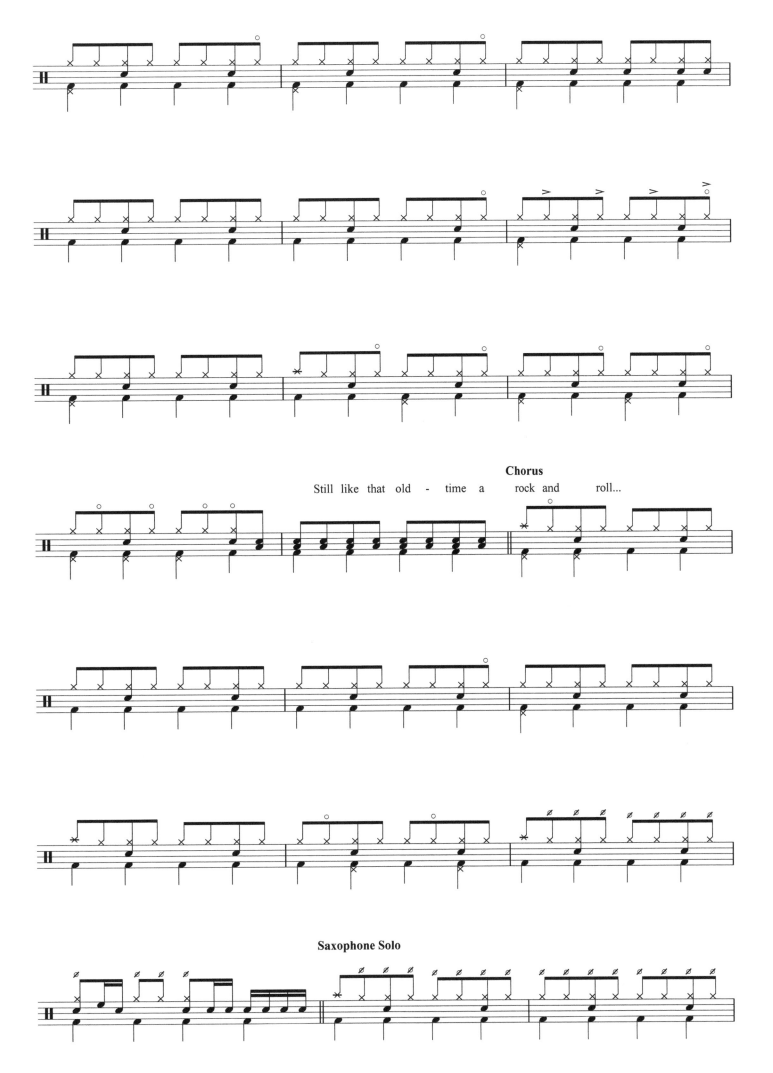

Chorus

Still like that old - time a   rock and   roll...

Saxophone Solo

Still like that old - time a

Chorus

rock and roll...

Still like that old - time a   rock and roll...

Breakdown-Chorus

Outro-Chorus

Begin fade   *Fade out*

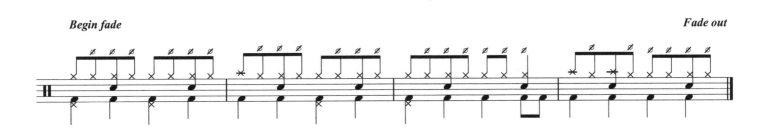

One Headlight

Words and Music by Jakob Dylan

Chorus

Come on, try a lit - tle, noth - ing is for - ev - er...

Play 3 times

Verse
Well, this place is old and feels just like a beat-up truck...

Play 3 times

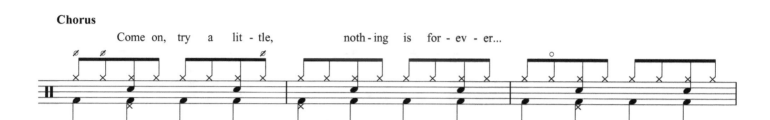

Chorus

Come on, try a lit - tle,   noth - ing is for - ev - er...

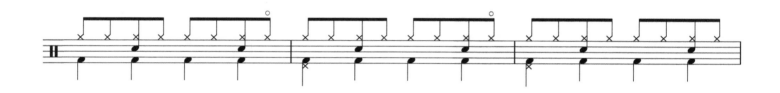

Outro

Repeat and fade

120

Rock and Roll All Nite

Words and Music by Paul Stanley and Gene Simmons

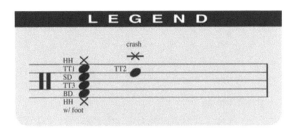

Pre-Chorus

You keep on shout - in'...

I

Chorus

wan - na   rock and   roll   all   nite...

Verse

You keep on say - in' you'll be mine for a while...

Pre-Chorus

You keep on shout - in'... I

Chorus

wan - na rock and roll all nite...

Guitar Solo

124

Pre-Chorus

You keep on shout - in'...

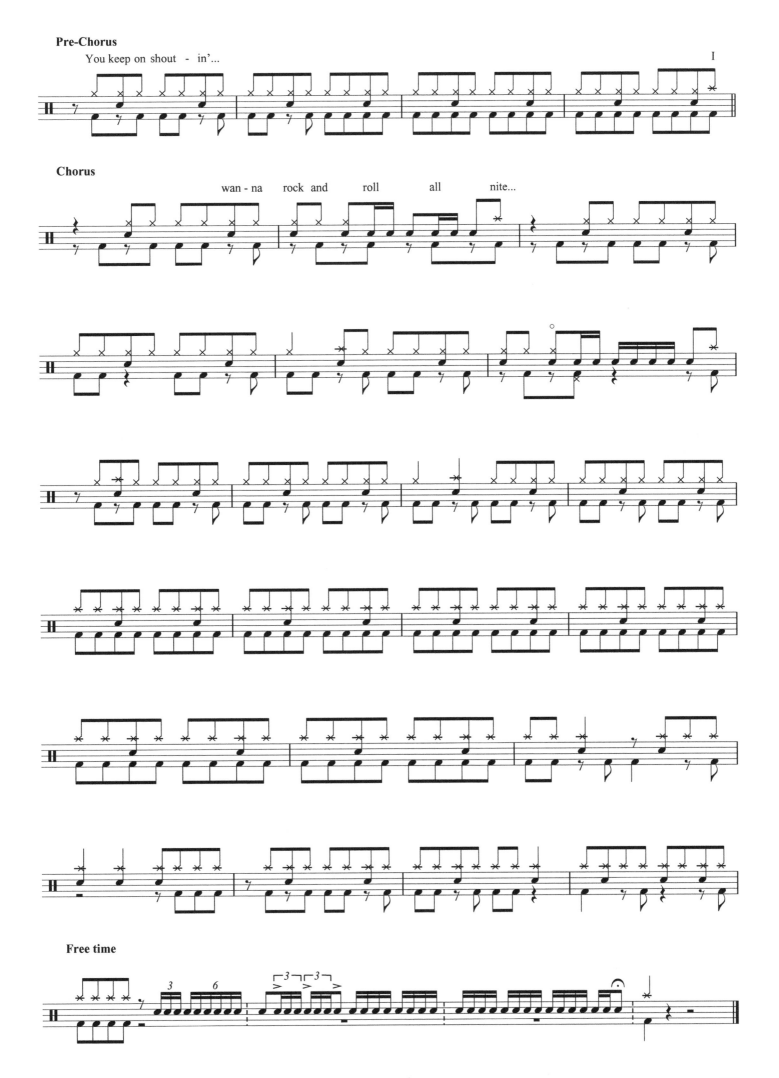

Chorus

wan - na   rock and   roll   all   nite...

Free time

Plush

Words and Music by Scott Weiland, Dean DeLeo,
Robert DeLeo and Eric Kretz

Pre-Chorus

Where ya go - in' for to - mor-row...

Interlude

Verse

Ah, and I feel so

much de-pends on the weath-er...

Bridge

And I feel it...

Pre-Chorus

Where ya go - in' for to - mor-row...

Chorus

When the dogs do find her...

Interlude

Pre-Chorus

Where ya go - in' for to - mor-row...

Chorus

When the dogs do find her...

Outro

Radioactive

Words and Music by Daniel Reynolds, Benjamin McKee,
Daniel Sermon, Alexander Grant and Josh Mosser

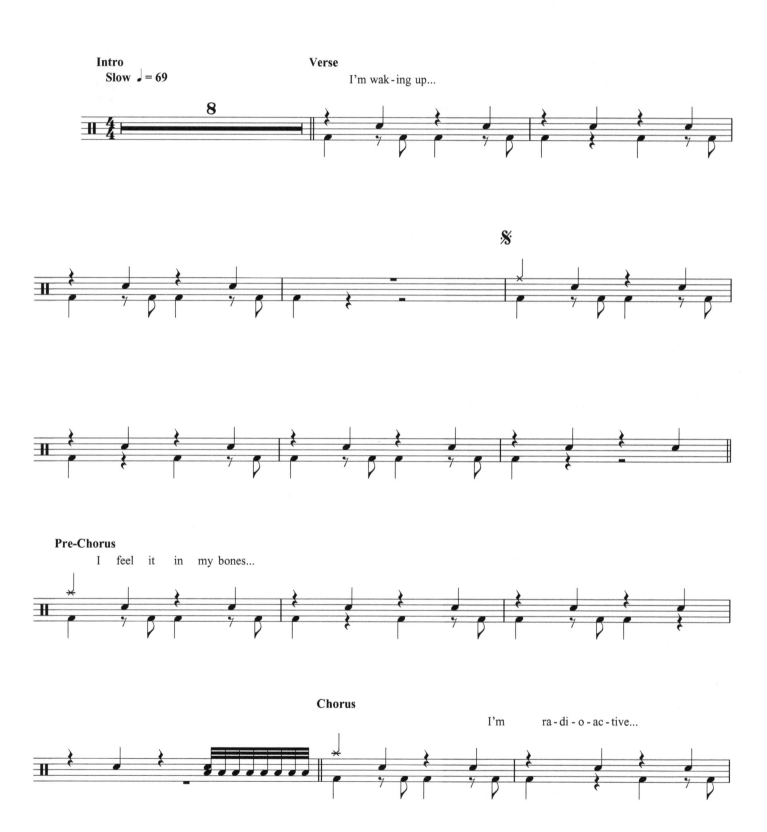

Verse

I raise my flag...

D.S. al Coda

⊕ **Coda**

Bridge

Pre-Chorus

I feel it in my bones...

Chorus

I'm

ra - di - o - ac - tive...

Seven Nation Army

Words and Music by Jack White

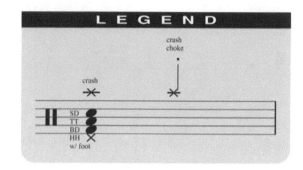

Intro
Moderately ♩ = 124

Verse

I'm gon - na   fight 'em off...

Play 4 times

Play 4 times

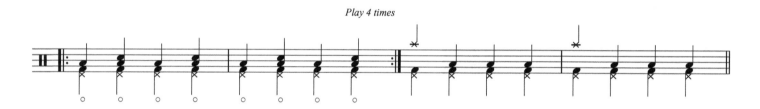

Interlude

Don't wan - na

Verse

hear a-bout it...

Guitar Solo

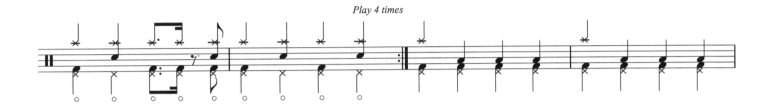

Verse

I'm go-in' to   Wich-i-ta...

Interlude

Sex and Candy

Words and Music by John Wozniak

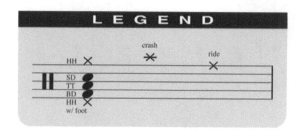

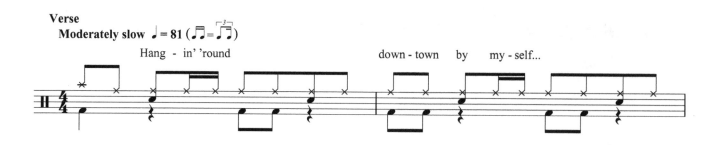

Hang - in' 'round   down - town   by   my - self...

Chorus

I smell sex and   can - dy...

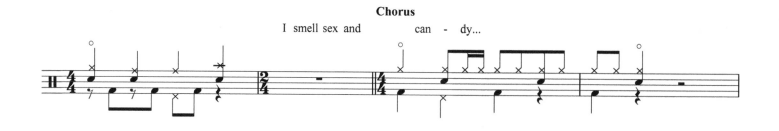

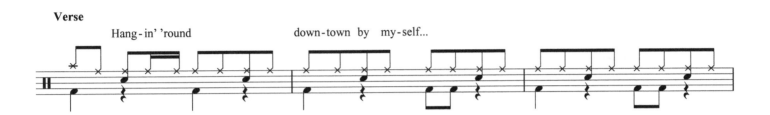

Verse

Hang-in' 'round   down-town by my-self...

I smell sex and

Chorus

can - dy...

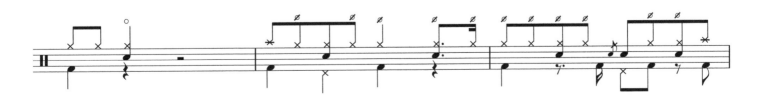

Chorus

I smell sex and   can - dy...

Sharp Dressed Man

Words and Music by Billy F Gibbons, Dusty Hill and Frank Lee Beard

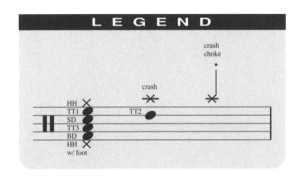

Intro
Moderate Rock ♩ = 124

Play 3 times

Verse
Clean   shirt...

Play 3 times

Chorus
They come   run - nin' just as   fast as they can...

Interlude

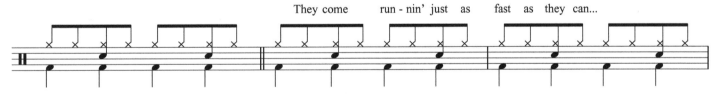

Verse
Gold   watch...

Play 3 times   *Play 6 times*

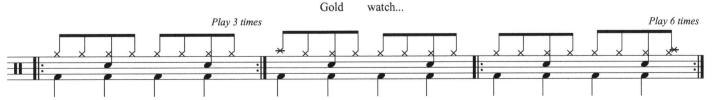

Chorus

They come   run - nin' just as   fast as   they can...

Guitar Solo

Play 8 times

Interlude

Play 6 times

Verse

Top   coat...

Play 7 times   *Play 7 times*

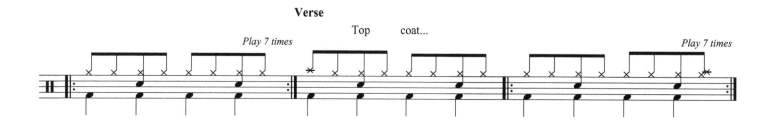

Chorus

They come   run - nin' just as   fast as   they can...

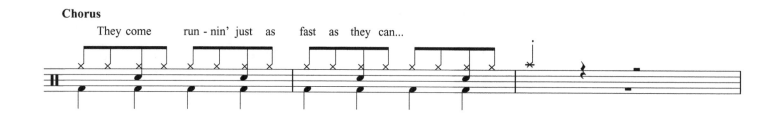

Outro-Guitar Solo

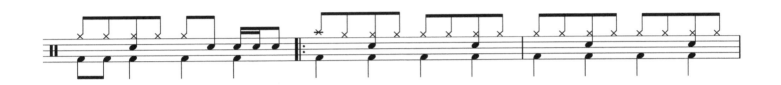

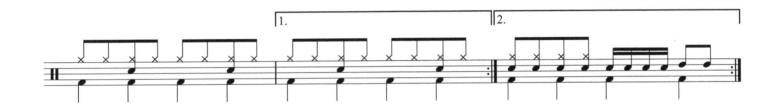

She's So Cold

Words and Music by Mick Jagger and Keith Richards

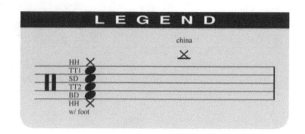

Intro
Moderately ♩ = 140

Verse

I'm so hot for her, I'm so hot for her...

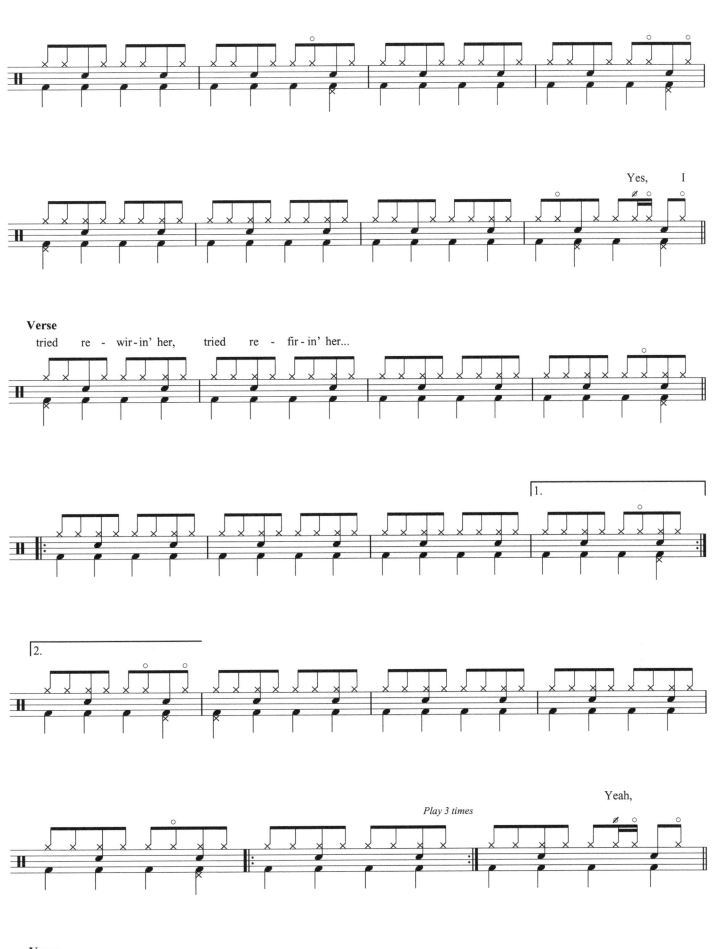

Yes,   I

Verse

tried   re - wir-in' her,   tried   re - fir - in' her...

1.

2.

Yeah,

Play 3 times

Verse

I'm   so   hot for her,   I'm   so   hot for her...

Play 5 times

Guitar Solo

She's

Verse

so cold, she's so cold...

Play 5 times

Verse

Who will be - lieve you were a beau - ty in - deed...

Begin fade

Fade out

144

Simple Man

Words and Music by Ronnie Van Zant and Gary Rossington

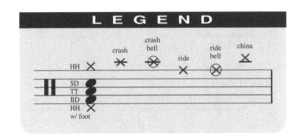

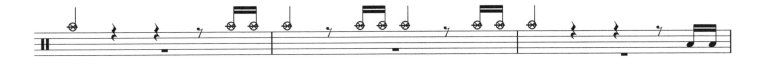

My ma - ma

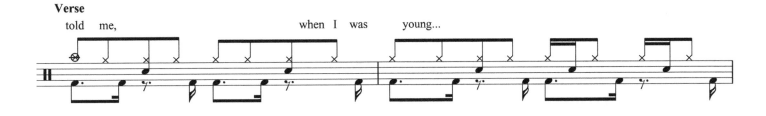

Verse

told me,   when I was   young...

Interlude

"Oh, take your

Verse

time,   don't live too fast...

And be a

Chorus

sim - ple   kind of man...

For - get your

Verse

lust   for the rich man's   gold...

And be a

sim - ple   kind   of   man...

To Coda

Guitar Solo

Oh, don't you

Verse

wor - ry,   you'll find your - self...

D.S. al Coda   Coda

And be a

Outro

Repeat and fade

Sunshine of Your Love

Words and Music by Eric Clapton, Jack Bruce and Pete Brown

Verse

I'm with you, my love...

Play 7 times

Play 3 times

Chorus

I've been wait - ing so long...

Guitar Solo

Verse

I'm   with you, my love...

Chorus

I've been wait - ing so long...

Play 3 times

Play 4 times

Repeat and fade

Sweet Child O' Mine

Words and Music by W. Axl Rose, Slash,
Izzy Stradlin', Duff McKagan and Steven Adler

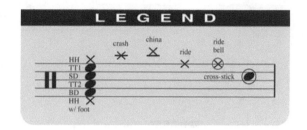

Intro
Moderate Rock ♩ = 122

Verse

She's got a smile that it seems to me...

2nd time, substitute Fill 1

2nd time, substitute Fill 2

2nd time, substitute Fill 2

Chorus

Whoa, whoa, whoa, sweet child of mine...

Fill 1

Fill 2

Guitar Solo

156

Chorus

Whoa,   oh,   oh,   oh,   sweet   child   of mine...

Guitar Solo

Outro

Where do we go?   Where do we go   now...

Free time

21 Guns

Words and Music by David Bowie, John Phillips,
Billie Joe and Green Day

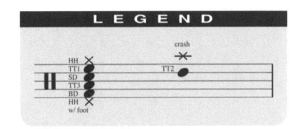

Intro
Slowly ♩ = 73

Verse
Moderately ♩ = 79

Does the pain weigh out the pride...

Play 3 times

Chorus

One, twen-ty-one guns...

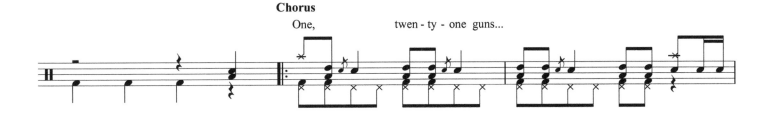

1.   2.

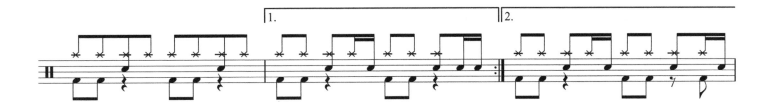

Verse

When you're at the

end of the road...

Play 5 times

Play 5 times

Chorus

One,   twen - ty - one guns...

Bridge

Did you try   to

live on your own...

Guitar Solo

Interlude   **Verse**

Chorus

One,   twen - ty - one guns...

3rd time, substitute Fill 1

1., 3.

2.

4.

Fill 1

Sweet Home Alabama

Words and Music by Ronnie Van Zant, Ed King and Gary Rossington

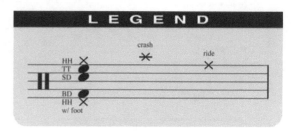

Verse

Big wheels keep on turn - in'...

Interlude

Verse

Well, I heard Mis-ter Young sing a-bout her...

Guitar Solo

Interlude

Verse

Now, Mus - cle Shoals has got the Swamp - ers...

1.

2.

D.S.S. al Coda 2

$\oplus$ Coda 2

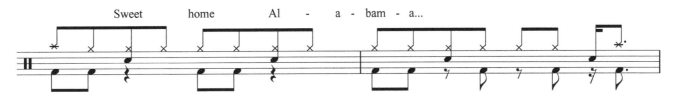

Sweet   home   Al - a - bam - a...

Outro

Begin fade

Fade out

Takin' Care of Business

Words and Music by Randy Bachman

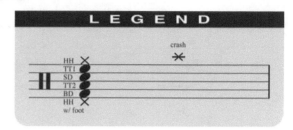

Intro
Moderate Rock ♩ = 126

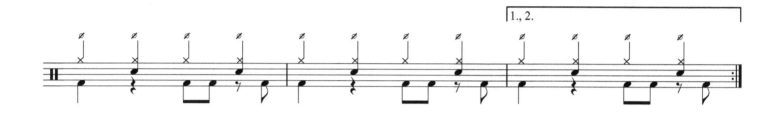

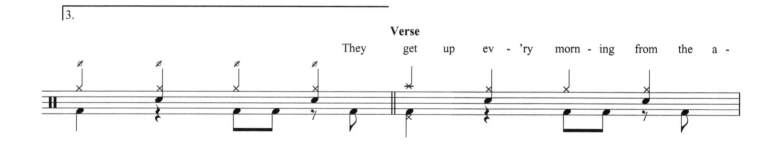

Chorus

tak - in' care of busi - ness...

Interlude

Verse

There's work   eas - y   as   fish - in'...

Chorus

And   we've been   tak - in' care of busi   -   ness...

Guitar Solo

Interlude

Bridge

Take good

care   of   my   busi - ness...

Guitar Solo

Play 3 times

Verse

They   get   up   ev - 'ry morn - ing from the a -

larm   clock's   warn - ing...

1.

2.

And   I've   been

Chorus

tak - in' care of busi - ness...

Play 3 times

Breakdown

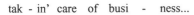

Tak - in' care of busi - ness...

Play 5 times

Outro

Tak - in' care of busi - ness...

Play 3 times

Repeat and fade

Thinking Out Loud

Words and Music by Ed Sheeran and Amy Wadge

Verse
Moderately slow ♩ = 79

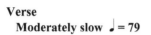

*Play 4 times

*Wire brushes on ride, drumstick on snare.

Pre-Chorus

peo - ple fall in love in mys - ter - i - ous ways...

Play 3 times

Chorus

So, hon - ey, now...

Play 4 times

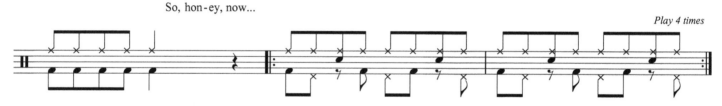

Verse

Pre-Chorus

peo - ple fall in love in mys - ter - i - ous ways...

Play 8 times *Play 3 times*

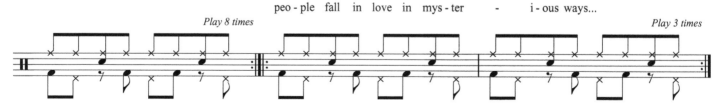

Chorus

That hon-ey, now...

Play 4 times

Guitar Solo

Play 3 times

Outro-Chorus

So, ba-by, now...

Play 4 times

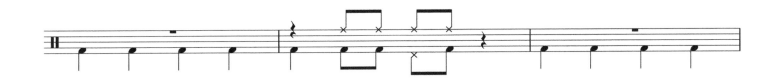

3AM

Lyrics by Rob Thomas
Music by Rob Thomas, Brian Yale,
John Leslie Goff and John Joseph Stanley

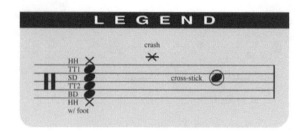

Intro
Moderately ♩ = 108

Verse

She says it's cold   out - side...

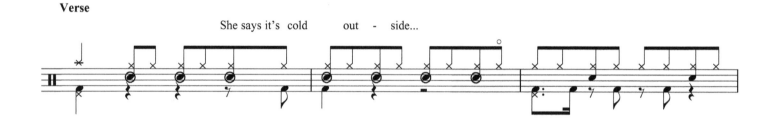

𝄋 **Chorus**

"Ba - by,   it's   three   a.   m..."

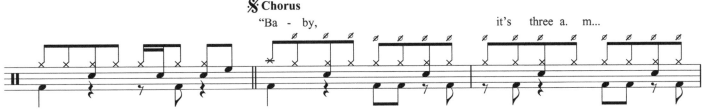

To Coda 2 𝄌   *To Coda 1* 𝄌

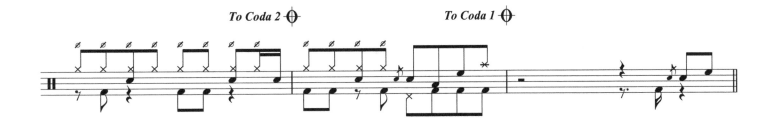

Interlude

Verse

But she's got a   lit - tle   bit of   some-thin'...

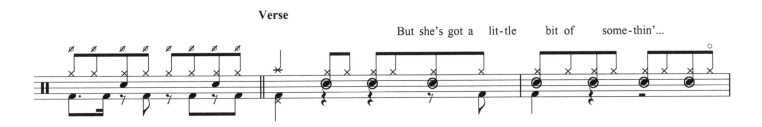

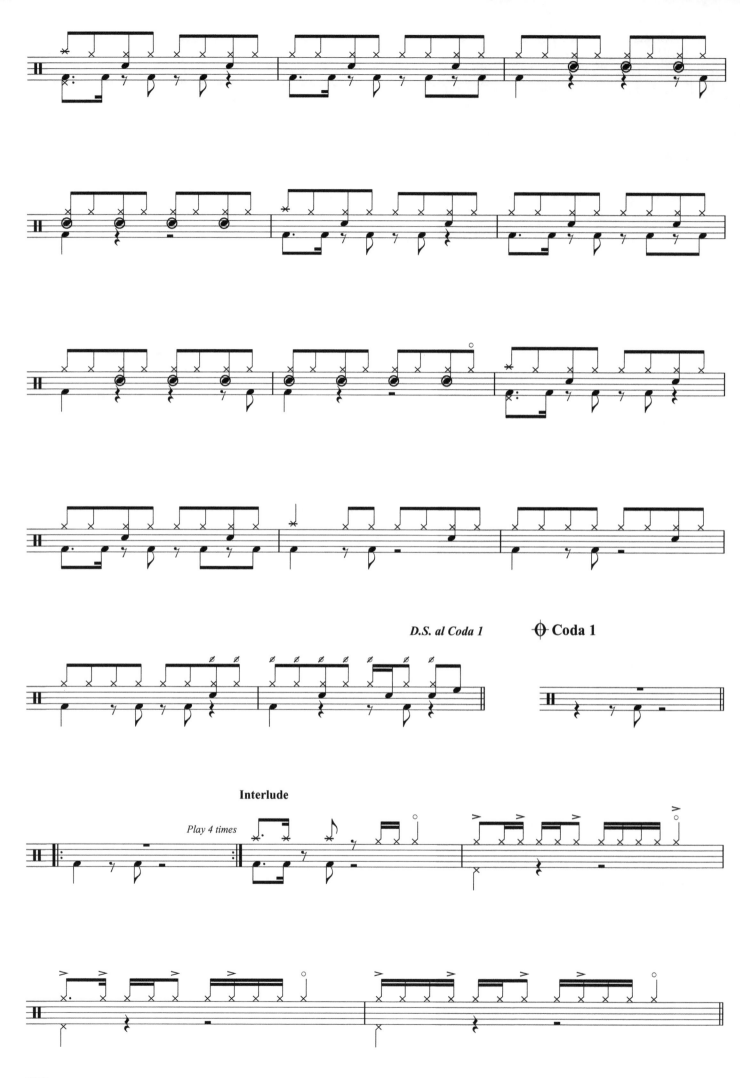

D.S. al Coda 1

Coda 1

Interlude

Play 4 times

Verse

Well, she be-lieves that life is made up...

Play 8 times

D.S. al Coda 2 ⊕ **Coda 2**

Yeah, but she says,

Outro

White Wedding

Words and Music by Billy Idol

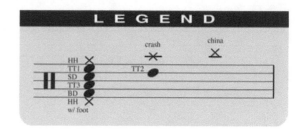

Intro
Moderately fast Rock ♩ = 144

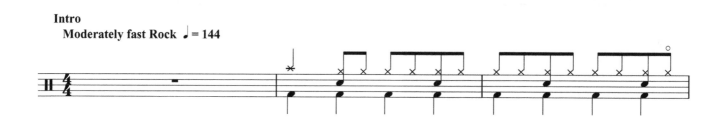

Verse

Hey, lit - tle sis - ter, what

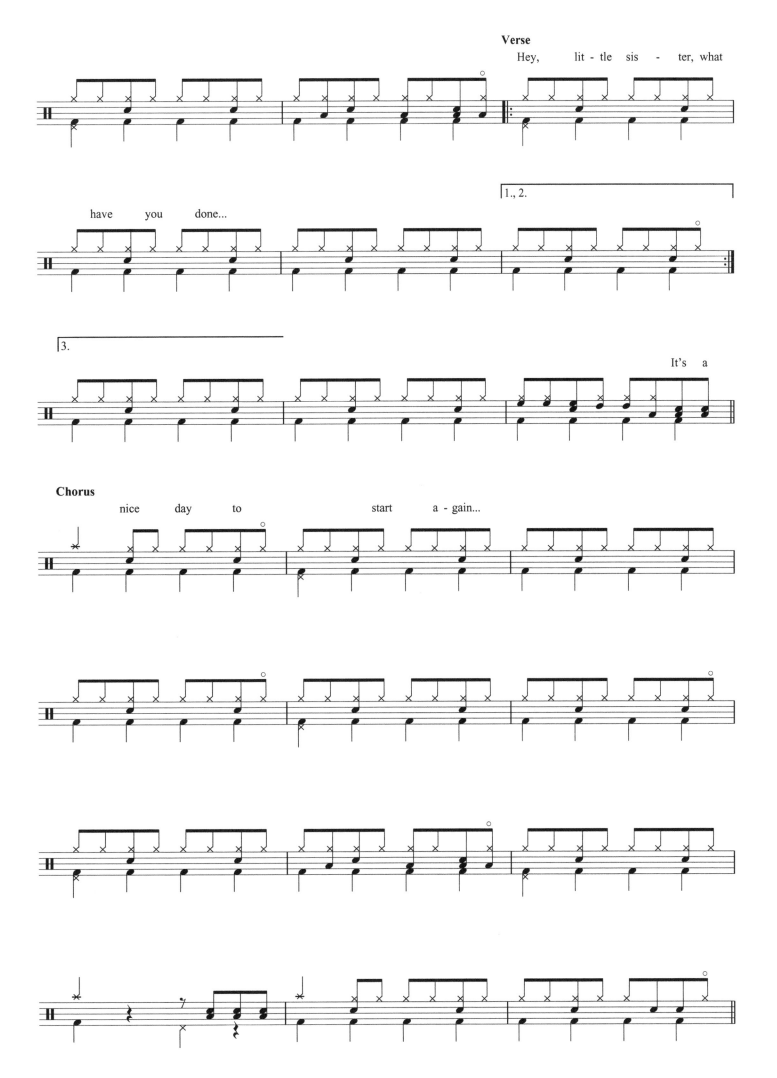

have you done...

1., 2.

3.

It's a

Chorus

nice day to start a - gain...

Verse

Hey, lit - tle sis - ter, who   is   it you're   with...

Chorus

It's   a   nice   day   to   start   a - gain...

Verse

Hey, lit - tle sis - ter, who

Interlude

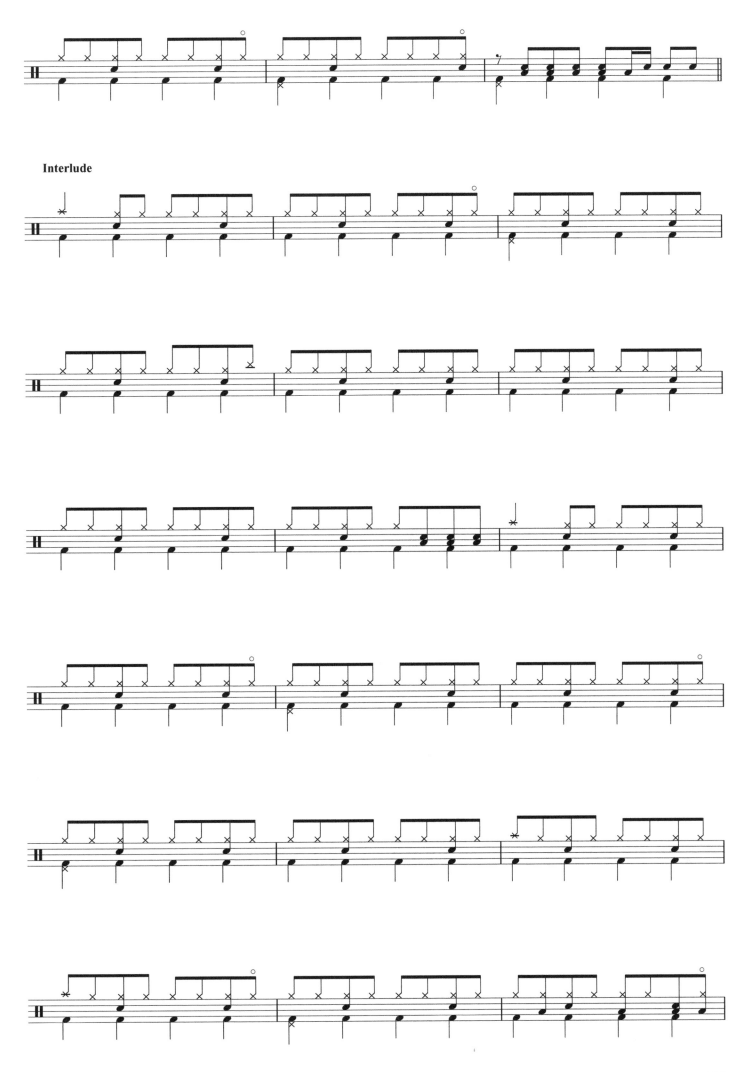

Verse

Hey,   lit - tle sis - ter, what   have   you   done...

1., 2.   3.

Chorus

It's a   nice   day   to

start   a - gain...

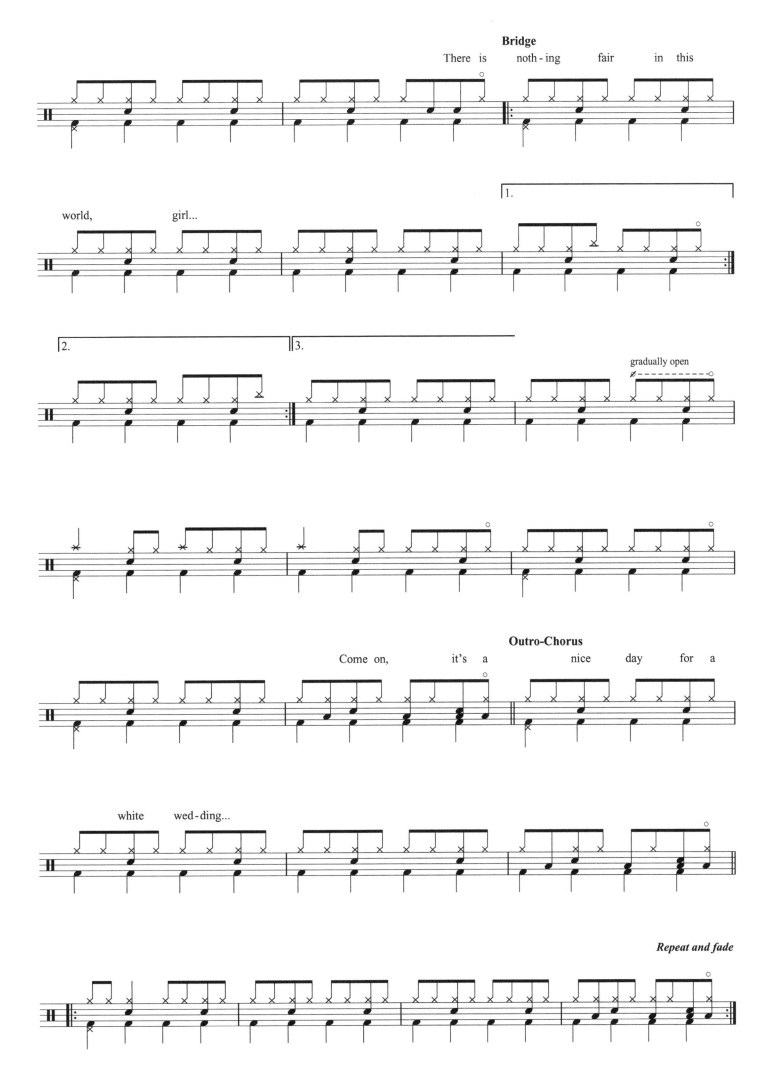

Bridge

There is noth-ing fair in this

world, girl...

1.

2. 3.

gradually open

Outro-Chorus

Come on, it's a nice day for a

white wed-ding...

Repeat and fade

With or Without You

Words and Music by U2

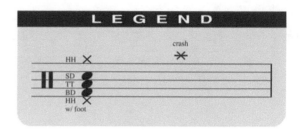

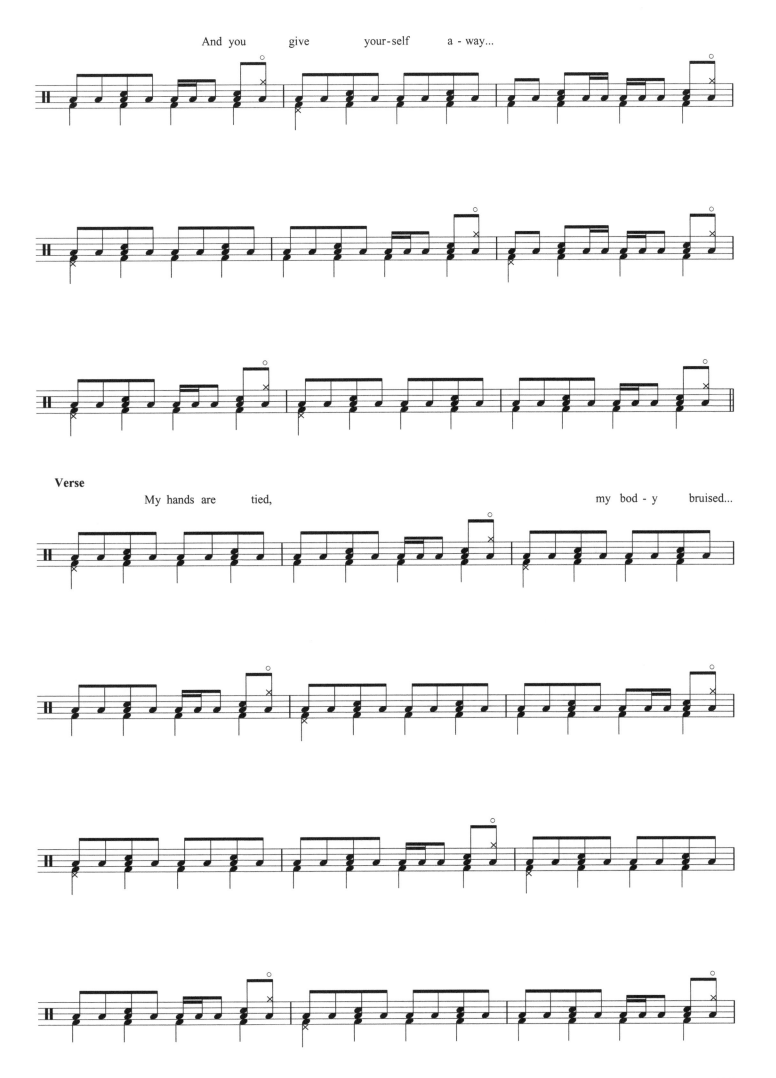

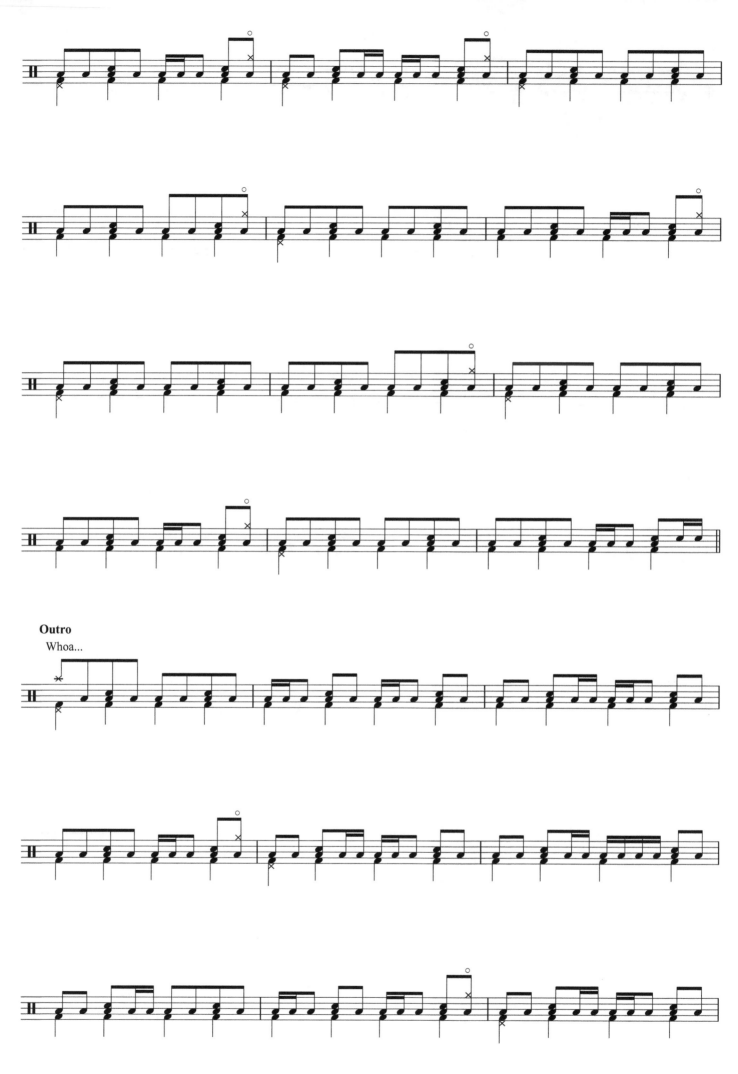

Outro

Whoa...

Begin fade

Fade out

DRUM PLAY-ALONG

AUDIO ACCESS INCLUDED

The Drum Play-Along™ Series will help you play your favorite songs quickly and easily! Just follow the drum notation, listen to the audio to hear how the drums should sound, and then play-along using the separate backing tracks. The lyrics are also included for reference. The audio files are enhanced so you can adjust the recording to any tempo without changing pitch!

HAL•LEONARD®

Visit Hal Leonard Online at
www.halleonard.com

Prices, contents and availability subject to change without notice and may vary outside the US.

YOU CAN'T BEAT OUR DRUM BOOKS!

Bass Drum Control
Best Seller for More Than 50 Years!
by Colin Bailey
This perennial favorite among drummers helps players develop their bass drum technique and increase their flexibility through the mastery of exercises.
06620020 Book/Online Audio $17.99

The Complete Drumset Rudiments
by Peter Magadini
Use your imagination to incorporate these rudimental etudes into new patterns that you can apply to the drumset or tom toms as you develop your hand technique with the Snare Drum Rudiments, your hand and foot technique with the Drumset Rudiments and your polyrhythmic technique with the Polyrhythm Rudiments. Adopt them all into your own creative expressions based on ideas you come up with while practicing.
06620016 Book/CD Pack $14.95

Drum Aerobics
by Andy Ziker
A 52-week, one-exercise-per-day workout program for developing, improving, and maintaining drum technique. Players of all levels – beginners to advanced – will increase their speed, coordination, dexterity and accuracy. The online audio contains all 365 workout licks, plus play-along grooves in styles including rock, blues, jazz, heavy metal, reggae, funk, calypso, bossa nova, march, mambo, New Orleans 2nd Line, and lots more!
06620137 Book/Online Audio $19.99

Drumming the Easy Way!
The Beginner's Guide to Playing Drums for Students and Teachers
by Tom Hapke
Cherry Lane Music
Now with online audio! This book takes the beginning drummer through the paces – from reading simple exercises to playing great grooves and fills. Each lesson includes a preparatory exercise and a solo. Concepts and rhythms are introduced one at a time, so growth is natural and easy. Features large, clear musical print, intensive treatment of each individual drum figure, solos following each exercise to motivate students, and more!
02500876 Book/Online Audio...............................$19.99
02500191 Book...$14.99

The Drumset Musician – 2nd Edition
by Rod Morgenstein and Rick Mattingly
Containing hundreds of practical, usable beats and fills, *The Drumset Musician* teaches you how to apply a variety of patterns and grooves to the actual performance of songs. The accompanying online audio includes demos as well as 18 play-along tracks covering a wide range of rock, blues and pop styles, with detailed instructions on how to create exciting, solid drum parts.
00268369 Book/Online Audio..................................$19.99

Instant Guide to Drum Grooves
The Essential Reference for the Working Drummer
by Maria Martinez
Become a more versatile drumset player! From traditional Dixieland to cutting-edge hip-hop, *Instant Guide to Drum Grooves* is a handy source featuring 100 patterns that will prepare working drummers for the stylistic variety of modern gigs. The book includes essential beats and grooves in such styles as: jazz, shuffle, country, rock, funk, New Orleans, reggae, calypso, Brazilian and Latin.
06620056 Book/CD Pack $12.99

1001 Drum Grooves
The Complete Resource for Every Drummer
by Steve Mansfield
Cherry Lane Music
This book presents 1,001 drumset beats played in a variety of musical styles, past and present. It's ideal for beginners seeking a well-organized, easy-to-follow encyclopedia of drum grooves, as well as consummate professionals who want to bring their knowledge of various drum styles to new heights. Author Steve Mansfield presents: rock and funk grooves, blues and jazz grooves, ethnic grooves, Afro-Cuban and Caribbean grooves, and much more.
02500337 Book..$14.99

Polyrhythms – The Musician's Guide
by Peter Magadini
edited by Wanda Sykes
Peter Magadini's *Polyrhythms* is acclaimed the world over and has been hailed by *Modern Drummer* magazine as "by far the best book on the subject." Written for instrumentalists and vocalists alike, this book with online audio contains excellent solos and exercises that feature polyrhythmic concepts. Topics covered include: 6 over 4, 5 over 4, 7 over 4, 3 over 4, 11 over 4, and other rhythmic ratios; combining various polyrhythms; polyrhythmic time signatures; and much more. The audio includes demos of the exercises and is accessed online using the unique code in each book.
06620053 Book/Online Audio..$19.99

Joe Porcaro's Drumset Method – Groovin' with Rudiments
Patterns Applied to Rock, Jazz & Latin Drumset
by Joe Porcaro
Master teacher Joe Porcaro presents rudiments at the drumset in this sensational new edition of *Groovin' with Rudiments*. This book is chock full of exciting drum grooves, sticking patterns, fills, polyrhythmic adaptations, odd meters, and fantastic solo ideas in jazz, rock, and Latin feels. The online audio features 99 audio clip examples in many styles to round out this true collection of superb drumming material for every serious drumset performer.
06620129 Book/Online Audio $24.99

66 Drum Solos for the Modern Drummer
Rock • Funk • Blues • Fusion • Jazz
by Tom Hapke
Cherry Lane Music
66 Drum Solos for the Modern Drummer presents drum solos in all styles of music in an easy-to-read format. These solos are designed to help improve your technique, independence, improvisational skills, and reading ability on the drums and at the same time provide you with some cool licks that you can use right away in your own playing.
02500319 Book/Online Audio...$17.99

DRUM TRANSCRIPTIONS
FROM HAL LEONARD

THE BEATLES DRUM COLLECTION

26 drum transcriptions of some of the Beatles' best, including: Back in the U.S.S.R. • Birthday • Can't Buy Me Love • Eight Days a Week • Help! • Helter Skelter • I Saw Her Standing There • Ob-La-Di, Ob-La-Da • Paperback Writer • Revolution • Sgt. Pepper's Lonely Hearts Club Band • Something • Twist and Shout • and more.

00690402 . . . .$19.99

BEST OF BLINK-182

Features Travis Barker's bashing beats from a baker's dozen of Blink's best. Songs: Adam's Song • Aliens Exist • All the Small Things • Anthem Part II • Dammit • Don't Leave Me • Dumpweed • First Date • Josie • Pathetic • The Rock Show • Stay Together for the Kids • What's My Age Again?

00690621 . . . .$22.99

DRUM CHART HITS

Authentic drum transcriptions of 30 pop and rock hits are including: Can't Stop the Feeling • Ex's & Oh's • Get Lucky • Moves like Jagger • Shake It Off • Thinking Out Loud • 24K Magic • Uptown Funk • and more.

00234062 . . . .$17.99

INCUBUS DRUM COLLECTION

Drum transcriptions for 13 of the biggest hits from this alt-metal band. Includes: Are You In? • Blood on the Ground • Circles • A Crow Left of the Murder • Drive • Megalomaniac • Nice to Know You • Pardon Me • Privilege • Stellar • Talk Shows on Mute • Wish You Were Here • Zee Deveel.

00690763 . . . .$17.95

BEST OF THE DAVE MATTHEWS BAND FOR DRUMS

Cherry Lane Music

Note-for-note transcriptions of Carter Beauford's great drum work: The Best of What's Around • Crash into Me • What Would You Say.

02500184 . . . .$19.95

DAVE MATTHEWS BAND – FAN FAVORITES FOR DRUMS

Cherry Lane Music

Exact drum transcriptions of every Carter Beauford beat from 10 of the most requested DMB hits: Crush • Dancing Nancies • Everyday • Grey Street • Jimi Thing • The Space Between • Tripping Billies • Two Step • Warehouse • Where Are You Going.

02500643 . . . .$19.95

METALLICA – ...AND JUSTICE FOR ALL

Cherry Lane Music

Drum transcriptions to every song from Metallica's blockbuster album, plus complete drum setup diagrams, and background notes on Lars Ulrich's drumming style.

02503504 . . . .$19.99

METALLICA – BLACK

Cherry Lane Music

Matching folio to their critically acclaimed self-titled album. Includes: Enter Sandman * Sad But True * The Unforgiven * Don't Tread On Me * Of Wolf And Man * The God That Failed * Nothing Else Matters * and 5 more metal crunchers.

02503509 . . . .$22.99

METALLICA – MASTER OF PUPPETS

Cherry Lane Music

Matching folio to the best-selling album. Includes: Master Of Puppets • Battery • Leper Messiah • plus photos.

02503502 . . . .$19.99

METALLICA – RIDE THE LIGHTNING

Cherry Lane Music

Matching folio to Metallica's second album, including: Creeping Death • Fade To Black • and more.

02503507 . . . .$19.99

NIRVANA DRUM COLLECTION

Features transcriptions of Dave Grohl's actual drum tracks on 17 hits culled from four albums: *Bleach, Nevermind, Incesticide* and *In Utero*. Includes the songs: About a Girl • All Apologies • Blew • Come as You Are • Dumb • Heart Shaped Box • In Bloom • Lithium • (New Wave) Polly • Smells like Teen Spirit • and more. Also includes a drum notation legend.

00690316 . . . .$22.99

BEST OF RED HOT CHILI PEPPERS FOR DRUMS

Note-for-note drum transcriptions for every funky beat blasted by Chad Smith on 20 hits from *Mother's Milk* through *By the Way*! Includes: Aeroplane • Breaking the Girl • By the Way • Californication • Give It Away • Higher Ground • Knock Me Down • Me and My Friends • My Friends • Right on Time • Scar Tissue • Throw Away Your Television • True Men Don't Kill Coyotes • Under the Bridge • and more.

00690587 . . . .$24.99

RED HOT CHILI PEPPERS – GREATEST HITS

Essential for Peppers fans! Features Chad Smith's thunderous drumming transcribed note-for-note from their *Greatest Hits* album. 15 songs: Breaking the Girl • By the Way • Californication • Give It Away • Higher Ground • My Friends • Scar Tissue • Suck My Kiss • Under the Bridge • and more.

00690681 . . . .$22.99

RED HOT CHILI PEPPERS – I'M WITH YOU

Note-for-note drum transcriptions from the group's tenth album: The Adventures of Rain Dance Maggie • Annie Wants a Baby • Brendan's Death Song • Dance, Dance, Dance • Did I Let You Know • Ethiopia • Even You Brutus? • Factory of Faith • Goodbye Hooray • Happiness Loves Company • Look Around • Meet Me at the Corner • Monarchy of Roses • Police Station.

00691168 . . . .$22.99

RUSH – THE SPIRIT OF RADIO: GREATEST HITS 1974-1987

17 exact drum transcriptions from Neil Peart! Includes: Closer to the Heart • Fly by Night • Freewill • Limelight • Red Barchetta • Spirit of Radio • Subdivisions • Time Stand Still • Tom Sawyer • The Trees • Working Man • 2112 (I Overture & II Temples of Syrinx).

00323857 . . . .$22.99

HAL•LEONARD®

7777 W. BLUEMOUND RD. P.O. BOX 13819 MILWAUKEE, WI 53213

www.halleonard.com

Prices, contents and availability subject to change without notice.